What is t
Marri
by Er

MW01292095

When I read Mr. Disney's book, *Marriage by Design*, I was overjoyed with his material! Being a Licensed Marriage and Family Therapist who does lots of integration with Christian theology, I found it to be insightful and "user friendly." The integration of scriptural truths with solid counseling concepts adds to its effectiveness.

> *Ron Hall*
> *Licensed Marriage and Family Therapist*
> *Board Certified Professional Christian Counselor*
> *Certified Trauma Specialist*
> *CCV Pastor of Encouragement*

"If, like many of us, you got married with the idea that love will make all things clear, do your relationship a favor and read *Marriage by Design*! Eric Disney does an amazing job of laying a biblical foundation for marriage and attacks "head on" the issues that have plagued couples for years."

> *Dale Harewood, Associate Pastor*
> *Covenant Blessing Fellowship, Wilmington, Ca.*

"Why wasn't this written two decades ago?" I believe that Eric Disney truly has the gift of imparting wisdom that is both sound and easy to implement. Its interactive nature allows couples to move beyond superficial texts that are quite common in this genre. I plan to utilize this book for couples that I work with in the future as well as recommend it to all of my colleagues as an excellent supplement to their marriage counseling."

> *Jay Fitter*
> *Licensed Marriage and Family Therapist*
> *Author, Respect Your Children*

Marriage by Design will take any couple to a higher level in their relationship roles as husband and wife and bless them in the process."

> *Mike Rodriguez, Senior Pastor*
> *Calvary Chapel Corona*

Prioritize Your Marriage
and you invest in the next
generation!

2 Cor 10:5

ERIC A. DISNEY

MARRIAGE
by Design

The Keys to Create,
Cultivate and Claim the
Marriage You've Always Wanted

outskirtspress
DENVER, COLORADO

Outskirts Press, Inc.
http://www.outskirtspress.com

Paperback ISBN: 978-1-4787-3691-2
Hardback ISBN: 978-1-4787-3692-9

Library of Congress Control Number: 2014909617

Outskirts Press and the "OP" logo are trademarks belonging to Outskirts Press, Inc.

PRINTED IN THE UNITED STATES OF AMERICA

This book is dedicated to
my beautiful wife, Jennifer,
whom God uses to show me much about marriage and myself.
To Denzel and Gerda, my father and mother,
who demonstrated a wonderful example of marital commitment,
and to Denny and Derek, Daddy's boys
and God's little reminders to me
that a healthy marriage is well worth the effort.

To Suzi Jones, whose heart for healing marriages was
an inspiration to others.

To Tony Malama, a gentle giant who through his example
taught me much about the importance of forgiveness.

Dad, Tony, and Suzi, your passings leave a hole in my heart

that will never be replaced. I take comfort in the knowledge

that I will see you all again.

I finally give thanks to those who showed great courage and
transparency
in sharing their personal stories within these pages
so that others might glean from the hope
that was given them.

Contents

Introduction
In the Beginning…

He stands in the local bookstore, perusing the most recent edition of a muscle magazine. He knows in the back of his mind that the only reason these guys were lucky enough to grace the pages was because the editors just hadn't seen him yet. Suddenly he senses someone staring him down. He cautiously glances to both sides. To the left, a short balding middle-aged man looking over a fine dining magazine; he seems oblivious. To the right, an older woman with her hair tied up in a conservative bun. She looks up and smiles, then goes back to reading her cross-stitching quarterly; it was surely not her.

He flips a couple of pages and again feels the stare. Looking up, he notices a pair of beautiful hazel eyes staring at him through the slot between the magazines on the rack. She quickly looks back to her magazine, but it is unmistakable: she was checking him out. Those exquisite hazel eyes are enough to call for further investigation. He subtly walks to the end of the aisle, making sure that she is not watching him. He walks around the end cap and there she stands. She is gorgeous, everything he has ever wanted in a woman. *She's the one!*

She glances up, hoping to catch another glimpse of him through the magazine rack. A look of sadness crosses her face as she lowers her head. He has gone.

"Hello," he says, nearly scaring her to death. She has been caught and looks quite embarrassed. "I'm sorry, I didn't mean to startle you," he adds, helping her save face. "I'm Mark."

"Hello, I was so engrossed in this article…my name is Sheila."

Their eyes lock, their hearts pound, their blood courses through their veins like a rushing river, the music swells…

Fifteen years later, in a dimly lit kitchen, Mark and Sheila sit at a table. I mention their names because if you could see them now you would never recognize them as the couple just described. They sit across from each other, no eye contact whatsoever. The tension is so thick you could cut it with a knife. You can hear the sound of a pesky fly whizzing about the room; the sound is bellowing in contrast to the dead silence in the room.

Not a word is spoken, but their body language speaks volumes. Mark is reading a newspaper on his laptop computer. Sheila stares into her coffee as she stirs it continuously, trancelike. The lines around her mouth suggest that the smile left her lips years ago. His eyebrows lower, as if the top of his nose were the only thing preventing them from sliding right off his face. He finishes his coffee, puts his laptop into its case, and heads toward the door. She glances up long enough to watch him leave the house. The sunny backlight from outside completely darkens his fading image as he shuts the door behind him. Once again the kitchen is dark, symbolic of the current status of their relationship. Not a word, not a smile, not a kiss, not even a "bye"—nothing. A scowl crosses her face. She looks back down at her coffee, giving it another pointless stir. What happened? What is going on?

Unfortunately, this is the picture of too many marriages. It doesn't take fifteen years for a marriage to collapse into a state of total disrepair. We have a pretty good idea what the next step will be for this marriage if something isn't done. Sadly, the statistics for divorce in this country are on the rise, and it's sobering to say that many who are reading this book right now may well be awaiting or have already served divorce papers.

So at this point, *what is the point*, you may be asking yourself. Ah, let's begin with a glimmer of hope regardless of your reason for picking up this book. The bad news is, you picked up this book. So what's the good news? You picked up this book. That shows there is a possibility of restoring and saving your marital commitment to one another. The most important thing to remember is that it takes two people to make a marriage work and two people to destroy a marriage. In very few instances a marriage dissolves solely because of the behaviors of just one spouse. Yet everyone who has ever come into my office has stated emphatically "it's *all their fault!*"

For others, perhaps you picked up this book because you've experienced some bumps in the road. Bumps are inevitable because every marriage consists of two different people, sometimes two *very* different people. The differences between us are what make a marriage exciting; we just have to figure out how to maneuver the waters of matrimony. Too many times couples didn't go through any type of premarital counseling so the actual marriage becomes the practice ground. I always tell couples to embrace their differences because if you had married someone exactly like yourself, one of you would have to die because the two of you could not exist in the same plane—you couldn't stand it over time!

And for yet others, perhaps you are contemplating marriage and want to learn a bit about building a solid marital foundation. If that is the case, God bless you. It is my sincere hope that there is something for everyone in what God allows me to unfold throughout this book. As with anything in life, having the tools and not actually using them can often constitute the problem in a nutshell. My prayer for all of you is that you would die to yourself and put forth the efforts necessary to create, cultivate, and claim the marriage that God has designed for you.

As a couple, it is greatly beneficial that you each have your own copy of this book. At various times you will be asked to do an individual assignment, while at other times you will be asked to work as a team on a given assignment. Obviously, if you are an individual reading this resource you will not be able to participate fully in the experience of this book, but you will receive great insight for that time when you have a partner with which to work through problems that will undoubtedly occur.

No marriage book will be able to address every situation in every marriage, but we will lay out a foundation for marriage based on my experience in working with couples for many years, as well as the foundation prescribed by the author of marriage himself, God. It is important that we go back to the source in assessing how effective we are in our marriage, and in making sure that the foundation is solid.

Imagine how frustrating it was when I tried to put together a little plastic tricycle for my son's second Christmas. The silly thing cost less than twenty dollars, so it must be easy to assemble, right? When I opened up the box the pieces just fell out. Breaking down the cost of this tricycle by the hundreds of pieces that fell on the floor, my first thought was that I got a great deal. Trouble however was looming on the horizon. First off, I'm no mechanical whiz. In fact, whatever the opposite of mechanical whiz happens to be, that's me. It wasn't long before heavy breathing, beads of sweat, and grunts of frustration all emanated from my very being as I tried to put this thing together.

I constantly referred to the picture on the box—you know, the perfectly assembled tricycle with a beaming little boy sitting on the seat, obviously proud of his competent father. Sad to say that this would not be the situation for my son Denny. Finally, defeated, angry, and exhausted, I pulled out the magic papers—the papers no man on earth should ever need: the dreaded instructions.

Yes, I reluctantly admitted that the instructions did make assembly much easier. As we walk through this journey together we will spend a lot of time referring to God's instruction manual for life and marriage, the Bible.

> All Scripture is God-breathed and is useful for teaching, rebuking, correcting and training in righteousness, so that the man of God may be thoroughly equipped for every good work.
>
> 2 Timothy 3:16-17

In this book you will find a variety of exercises concluding each chapter called "Taking Action" that I recommend you take seriously and actually write out. You must remember we are trying to establish a new pattern of behavior in your marital relationship. Spending the time writing will move some of what you may have been experiencing emotionally from a "feeling" state to a "thinking" state, getting you to a place where you can begin to assess and make changes. It's difficult to sort things out when they are tied up in an emotional bundle. There will be times when you will be requested to go on scripture runs and look up and write down some scriptural references. It's important to begin to use your Bible and discover what the intent of marriage truly is.

You will see a smattering of personal testimonies throughout the book, sections titled "In Their Own Words" designed to show practical application of the various topics discussed. These testimonies will offer hope to couples regardless of the extent to which their marriage may be in crisis. They will also serve as warning signs to those who have been slipshod in their marriages up to this point. We have also not heard the last of Mark and Sheila as excerpts from their lives will introduce some of the chapters in this book to serve as impetus for growth in our personal relationships.

Every chapter ends with a section for personal notes, a place for you to jot down the concepts, thoughts, and/or scriptures that really spoke to you in that chapter. By doing so, you will end each chapter with your own personal footnotes for use as a quick reference when necessary.

The first objective is to establish a foundation for hope, faith, and trust. For some of you, restoration of your marital commitment will be a longer process than it is for others. The decision to change can be immediate, but healthier behaviors and healing will occur over time. How dedicated you are to your relationship will be in direct proportion to the amount of time and speed with which you heal and grow.

We will begin our journey examining the basic question: "What is my marriage supposed to look like?" Without a clear understanding of the institution of marriage it is very difficult to benchmark the direction in which we are headed. Let's examine the model of marriage.

Part I:

Laying the Foundation

Chapter One

What Is My Marriage Supposed to Look Like?

Fourteen years earlier, Sheila sits at a quaint little table just outside a local sandwich shop.

"Sheila!" She looks up from her menu and rises as Mark approaches. Mark gives her a big kiss and they sit. "You know, I love this place but they need to do something about the parking. This is crazy! I was driving around for twenty minutes just to get a spot two blocks away," Mark sputters between deep breaths.

Sheila smiles. "Obviously someone needs to work harder at the gym."

Mark checks out the menu. "Good day?"

"Yeah, it's been okay."

He looks up from his menu with suspicion. "What happened?"

"It was nothing bad, really. I've just been spending a lot of time thinking about something that Claire from work mentioned."

Mark has a quirky smile on his face, hoping to move the conversation forward. "And?"

After a momentary pause, Sheila continues. "She was just talking. They've been getting premarital counseling. I guess the counselor is laying out a complete foundation for them. She says it has been helping them to talk to each other better and really understand what their marriage commitment is going to be about."

"Honey, we're not talking rocket science here. We've been married for almost a year, and I think we're doing well." Mark smiles at her. "I don't understand what's got you all bound up."

"Listen, I'm not saying that we're having these major problems. That's not it. You know how we can butt heads from time to time. It might not be a bad idea to talk to someone or at least, I don't know, maybe do a marriage study together." Sheila shrugs, uncertain how she will be received.

Mark looks puzzled. He shakes his head. "Come on, you're taking this way too seriously."

A bit offended by his nonchalance, Sheila says in a quiet voice, "My marriage is serious."

Mark realizes that he has hurt her. "Sheila, I take our marriage very seriously. I love you. I married you in the sight of God and promised to take care of you. I meant that."

"I just want our marriage to be great. I don't want us to end up like my mom and dad."

Mark smiles. "I think we have a solid foundation. I think we're doing what we are supposed to be doing."

"I don't want to think, I want to know."

Our society has done such an effective job of distorting the concept and institution of marriage. No wonder couples are confused going into marriage. We will begin laying the foundation for marriage by examining the opening question, "What is my marriage supposed to look like?" We will identify what the design of marriage is and how it should be executed based on what Scripture says—essentially discovering the direction we should be headed and assessing the detours that may have occurred along the way. The ultimate goal is to get back on track and move in the right direction.

When taking back ground, doubt and frustration often arise, making this an ideal time to offer some meditation verses to move you forward and serve as a reminder that you are not alone in this endeavor. Refer to this list as often as necessary, and commit these verses to heart and mind.

FOR MEDITATION AND ENCOURAGEMENT

> Trust in the Lord with all your heart, and lean not on your own understanding; in all your ways acknowledge him, and he will make your paths straight.
>
> Proverbs 3:5-6

> Call upon me in the day of trouble; I will deliver you, and you will honor me.
>
> Psalm 50:15

> Blessed is he whose help is the God of Jacob, whose hope is in the Lord his God, the Maker of heaven and earth, the sea, and everything in them—the Lord who remains faithful forever.
>
> Psalm 146:5-6

> Fear not, for I have redeemed you; I have called you by name; you are mine. When you pass through the waters I will be with you; and when you pass through the rivers, they will not sweep over you; when you walk through the fire, you will not be burned; the flames will not set you ablaze. For I am the Lord, your God, the Holy One of Israel, your Savior.
>
> Isaiah 43:1-3

The Lord is good, a refuge in times of trouble. He cares for those who trust in him.

Nahum 1:7

May the God of hope fill you with all joy and peace as you trust in him, so that you may overflow with hope by the power of the Holy Spirit.

Romans 15:13

No temptation has seized you except what is common to man. And God is faithful; he will not let you be tempted beyond what you can bear. But when you are tempted, he will also provide a way out so that you can stand up under it.

1 Corinthians 10:13

[God]…is able to do immeasurably more than all we ask or imagine, according to his power that is at work within us.

Ephesians 3:20

We have this hope as an anchor for the soul, firm and secure. It enters the inner sanctuary behind the curtain, where Jesus, who went before us, has entered on our behalf. He has become a high priest forever, in the order of Melchizedek.

Hebrews 6:19-20

Now, equipped with some ammunition, let's enter the battlefield together.

Many couples do not seek premarital counsel prior to making their lifelong commitment before God, and that includes self-proclaimed Christians. As a professional counselor, I can tell you that premarital counseling is far more fun and exciting than sitting down with a couple who has been married for ten years (or more) with divorce the daily topic of conversation or, worse yet, the divorce papers have already been filed! The latter scenario is much more difficult to work through, not to say that it's impossible. Reconciliation is very possible when couples decide to rededicate themselves to their marriages and one another. Be encouraged, do not lose hope! We serve a big God who wants nothing more than to heal the pain and hurt, to heal your marriage and redeem your commitment.

MARRIAGE IS…

So what is marriage? Let's define it, shall we?

Marriage is a gift given by God to his creation. In Genesis 2:18-25, the story of creation talks about the need for man (Adam) to have a suitable helper. God did not want man to be alone so he created a partner suitable in Eve. You'll note that God created man out of Adam's rib; woman is a part of man, a very important part that was designed to fulfill a healthy need.

Marriage was designed to be a permanent commitment to one another before God.

> For this reason a man will leave his father and mother and be united to his wife, and the two will become one flesh. So they are no longer two, but one. Therefore what God has joined together, let man not separate.
>
> Matthew 19:5-6

It's the idea of taking two pieces of plywood and gluing them together. Once the glue has set, try to separate the two sheets. It's impossible to do so without causing irreparable damage to both pieces of wood. You will also note in this passage that Jesus speaks of leaving father and mother. Couples are to be bound to one another, with God as the glue. This is why there are often problems when one spouse wants their family to be the other partner in the relationship rather than the spouse they married. This causes nothing but dissention and can undermine the marriage commitment. There is nothing wrong with input from the in-laws, but do not give them sole authority in the relationship with your mate. Let them attend to their own marriages; you attend to yours.

To solidify God's intention that marriage be permanent, read Romans 7:2-3. God's intent was that, ideally, death should be the only circumstance that dissolves a marriage. He means for marriage to be a lifelong commitment.

Marriage is an opportunity to learn how to love another. For many, this is no small task. Depending on our background and upbringing, we may not have had love demonstrated to us. This can make it very difficult when we try to show someone the love that we never received. It becomes important to understand and accept that God loves us unconditionally. There is nothing we can do to earn it. God's love is a free gift, no strings attached.

> For God so loved the world that he gave his one and only Son, that whoever believes in him shall not perish but have eternal life.
>
> John 3:16

Can you possibly imagine sacrificing your child for the good of another? This wonderfully summarizes how much God has done for us and how much he truly loves his creation.

Marriage is not exempt from suffering. Some of you may be saying to yourself, "Marital suffering, that I understand. I've done plenty of it!"

> The Spirit himself testifies with our spirit that we are God's children. Now if we are children, then we are heirs—heirs of God and co-heirs with Christ, if indeed we share in his sufferings in order that we may also share in his glory.
>
> Romans 8:16-17

In your marriage, remember that when one of you suffers, you both suffer. Our responsibility is to be of support and encouragement to our mates. Plenty of people are willing to tear you down, but you should never be your partner's enemy, for you are called to be a team. This is not to say that marriage does not hold times of great joy and gladness (Jeremiah 33:11). Marriage has the potential to be one of the most gratifying decisions you will ever make.

Marriage sets the best example to children, and it is in this context that they should be raised ideally. Modeling a healthy marriage is the greatest gift you can give your children, who in all likelihood will take the same journey as their parents.

> Has not the Lord made them one? In flesh and spirit they are his. And why one? Because he was seeking godly offspring. So guard yourself in your spirit, and do not break faith with the wife of your youth.
>
> Malachi 2:15

What example are you setting in your marriage? Sons look to their fathers to learn how a man is to behave. Daughters watch their mothers very closely to determine the best ways to interact with the opposite sex. If petty bickering, infidelity, verbal abuse, and constant talk of divorce is your model, you will see the same patterns on display in their own relationships. Children learn well and will follow your example if they don't choose to do something about it. Consider: how often do you respond based on the example that you were shown growing up? As parents, we are always being observed. Remember that!

Marriage is a public demonstration of Christ and the church to people who may never set foot in church. Your marriage sets an example to others. Ephesians 5:23 states, "For the husband is the head of the wife as Christ is the head of the church, his body of which he is the Savior. Now as the church submits to Christ, so also wives should submit to their husbands in everything."

Ladies, don't get your feathers ruffled just yet. We'll shed greater light on this passage further into this chapter. We will lay out the entire marital roles and explore how and why Ephesians 5:23 works. Back to topic, are you setting an example for others to follow?

Marriage is designed to be an honorable endeavor.

> Marriage should be honored by all, and the marriage bed kept pure, for God will judge the adulterer and all the sexually immoral. Keep your lives free from the love of money and be content with what you have, because God has said, "Never will I leave you; nor forsake you."
>
> Hebrews 13:4-5

Do you set an honorable example? Do you display integrity in your relationship? Are you a man or woman of your word? We demonstrate great hypocrisy if we teach and proclaim a certain set of moral or ethical values, yet behind closed doors we do not live up to those beliefs. How much more troubling when we represent God to the world around us yet lead a double life of selfish desire. The person who acknowledges the damage pornography can have on a marriage but continues to gratify themselves on the Internet does not display godly integrity. Again we come back to the example we are setting in our marriage: an example to our children, our families, and the world.

Marriage is the perfect environment to cultivate romance. The entire concept of love has been so twisted and warped by our society that many don't know the difference between love and lust. Merriam-Webster defines lust as "intense or unbridled sexual desire: lasciviousness." Further defining lasciviousness we read "lewd, lustful." The synonyms include bawdy, coarse, crude, filthy, indecent, and obscene to list a few. The antonyms include clean, decent, and wholesome. The same source definition of love states, "strong affection for another arising out of kinship or personal ties, attraction based on sexual desire: affection and tenderness." Synonyms include "attachment, devotion, admiration, fondness and passion." Antonyms listed are "hate, hatred, and loathing."

Love has become a "no strings attached proposition," all about the momentary physical pleasure with little or no regard for the other(s) involved in the sex act. There is a distinct difference between "making love" and "having sex." The difference involves what motivates those involved. The act of making love in a committed relationship involves respect, selflessness, and communication. For those who are unaware, I would encourage you and your spouse to sit down together and read through Song of Songs. You will discover one of the most beautiful stories of love and affirmation in all of Scripture. This book unfolds the story of a bride and her bridegroom exploring their love for one another and their love for God.

Of course these are not the only scriptures that offer guidance as to the design for marriage, but they will certainly give a solid foundation to start.

DEALING WITH THE "S" WORD (SUBMISSION)

As we continue our journey let's entertain a topic that is bound to raise the hackles of some wives. The issue of submission has been so distorted that it has lost all of its original meaning, certainly as laid out scripturally and how it applies to the relationship between a husband and wife. Let's give it some clarification; we will not dilute the meaning to make it more palatable but simply brush away all the assumptions and misconceptions to expose what God truly means by submission.

It is fascinating how even men who spend very little time reading the Bible have the following scripture committed to heart.

> Wives, submit to your husbands, as is fitting to the Lord.
>
> Colossians 3:18

Ladies, some of you didn't like reading it a few pages back in the reference to Ephesians 5:22-23, and you may not be thrilled to hear it again, but follow me for a few moments before slamming the book shut. Husbands, you listen as well! First of all, if Scripture mentions something more than once, pay attention to it. When we look at submission it is imperative that we examine the flow of the marital roles, how they work together, and how they are unique. (Figure 1.1) The model starts with God at the top, for he is the designer of marriage and all creation. The next two elements (husband and wife) are not ordered in importance but rather differentiated by responsibility of role. Galatians 3:28-29 makes it clear that in God's eyes we are all equal.

What we know about God is that he loves both the husband and the wife equally with no qualifications. He has at heart the best interest of both people in the marriage. Ephesians 5:23 declares that the husband is the head of the wife. "Are you saying that he is my boss?" the wives may be asking. No, not at all, ladies. What it means is that God has given men a role that is unique to them. Within the context of marriage, the husband is called to be the spiritual leader of the household.

Ah, here is often where the issue of submission becomes derailed. Husbands, take a moment and assess your effectiveness

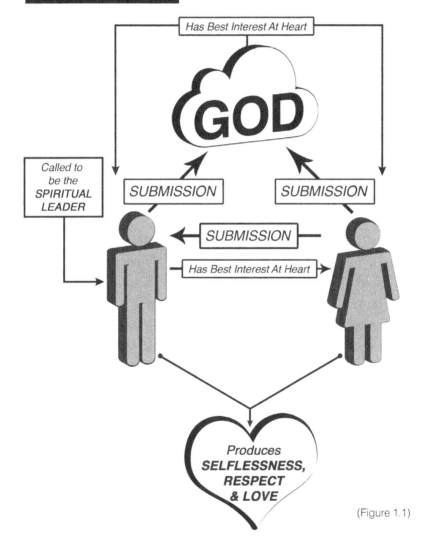

(Figure 1.1)

as the spiritual leader. Are you leading your family in the ways of God? Do you as the spiritual leader demonstrate God to your household? Does your family know that you have their best interest at heart? Do you attend church with the family, demonstrating that it has priority? Don't expect it to have priority with your children if it has none with you. Are you praying with and for your wife and family? Are you in fellowship with others?

There are many ways to demonstrate the spiritual aspect of our being to our family. If you are weak in this area it will affect your credibility as the leader and the willingness of your family to follow you. Men, stated simply, you are called to treat your wife and family in the same manner that God treats you. It is a tall order, and if you are not tapped into Scripture and cultivating a relationship with Him, you will not know how to lead.

UNDERSTANDING THE ROLES

When talking to men who struggle to lead their families, often I will ask them how their fathers modeled manhood to them. Many times they concede that they have had to figure it out for themselves because Dad was either always working, too busy, emotionally unavailable, distant from their wives, or even had affairs scattered on the horizon. None of which sets a great example. Bottom line, they had no earthly model. Guys, our God wants to be that model for you. We need to develop a close relationship with God so that we can have a healthy relationship with our wives and children.

Men, if someone is talking to you in a normal tone of voice from an office six doors down, are you likely to hear them? If you walk down to their office and continue the conversation, naturally you are going to hear what they have to say. The same goes with our relationship to God. Draw close to God and let him show you how to lead your family spiritually. In this way you can fulfill God's calling on your life. You have a greater accountability to God by the design of your role in marriage. Your goal is to live up to it to the best of your ability.

As to women, wives are called to be submissive, by virtue of their role, to their husbands, and the husbands are called to treat their wives and family as God treats him. Submission for the wife involves being a support to her husband. God knew it was necessary that Adam have a suitable helper so he fashioned one out of a part of Adam, his rib. The passage from Genesis 2:20-24 is the well-known foundation for the woman's role. It is evident that the woman was needed to complete the man; they complement one another. She is called to be an encouraging, loving, and trusting support to her mate. She is called to show loyalty and confidence in her husband.

The biblical design for marriage is entirely countercultural as the media portrays the head of most households to be incompetent buffoons not receiving and apparently totally undeserving of the respect of either their spouse or children. Scripturally, the wife is called to do nothing to jeopardize her support of her man. Proverbs 31:10-31 addresses the character qualities necessary to fulfill this very important role, and the value of a "virtuous woman" is described in this passage as: "She is worth far more than rubies." Men, keep that in mind, and treat them as such!

I guess the real question is, "Wives, why wouldn't you be willing to be submissive if your spouse was fulfilling his role and modeling God's love to you?" Submission probably wouldn't even be an issue if everyone were fulfilling their roles.

> Husbands, love your wives and do not be harsh with them. Children, obey your parents in everything, for this pleases the Lord. Fathers, do not embitter your children, or they will become discouraged.
>
> Colossians 3:19-21

Did you notice? Men are equally bound by submission. In fact, submission begins with the husband by virtue of his role. Paul states in Ephesians 5:1-2, "Be imitators of God, therefore, as dearly loved children and live a life of love, just as Christ loved us and gave himself up for us as a fragrant offering and sacrifice to God." He continues his thought in verse 21, "Submit to one another out of reverence for Christ." The evidence displayed by our Savior through his selfless sacrifice exemplifies his love for us.

The husband is called to honor God out of respect for who he is and by merit of his title, creator of all things and designer of life. This is a foundation for reverence as denoted in the above scripture. His is the example to follow as demonstrated in the life of Jesus Christ. Our call to submission is an observance of role and title, but it is not the only reason.

LEADING FROM CHARACTER

Interestingly, God does not lead from his position of authority, he leads from his character. Many of these qualities we are called to emulate as his creation. However, some of God's character qualities are not passed down to his creation, including omnipresence (is everywhere), omniscience (all-knowing), and eternal (always existed and not bound by time).

Some other attributes, including wrath and jealousy, do not show that God loves us any less. The fact that he detests sin only serves to prove that he wants what is best for us. He knows what sin produces in his creation. As with any good father, just discipline is the consequence of a child's bad behavior. Character attributes that we can experience include wisdom (Job 12:13), faithfulness, truth (Titus 1:2), mercy (Exodus 34:6), grace (Romans 3:23-24), patience (Psalm 103:8), peace (1 Corinthians 14:33), and righteousness (Deuteronomy 32:4) to name a few.

God offers us free will, the choice to follow his lead and live out these character qualities. As most of us do not respond well to dictates, God leads from the characteristics that show his love, grace, and mercy. As Christians we are called to share God and his Word in love, the way Jesus did. As husband and wife we are called to personify those same characteristics that God shows in his love for us.

When a married couple adheres to their responsibility, the outcome is rewarding. Showing the appropriate regard for our God-given roles produces in our relationship the same attitude as exhibited toward God. What is produced is selflessness, respect, and love for one another in marriage. Is there a better example to set for your children?

First Peter 3:7 calls you husbands to treat your wives in a respectful manner so that nothing will hinder your relationship with God. God has given your wives a unique temperament, the ability to think and reason, and the same grace and mercy that he extends to you. Do not treat them as second-class citizens. Their role of support and contribution is equally important, albeit different from yours.

Men, respect and listen to your wives. They are allowed to present suggestions and opinions in a loving way. God didn't say that man is the smarter one. Your differences complement each other. Where one is strong often the other shows weakness and vice versa. The marital relationship should not be deemed a competition but rather a cooperative.

In the example of the two sheets of plywood, the strength of the two sheets now glued together is considerably greater than either one was individually, and so it is with marriage. Marriage is one of the few times in life that one plus one can equal three. There is far greater benefit in working together than would be evident in each of you working individually.

When I'm counseling a couple and the wife appears to be the more aggressive partner, it usually means the husband is taking the passive role and not leading the home spiritually. In too many cases, the wife is the one who takes the kids to church and grows the family spiritually. This is not the role of the wife, but praise God someone is willing to step up. If this is the case in your relationship, I encourage the man to stand up and take his rightful role. It won't be easy, because your wife has to develop the trust necessary to relinquish that role. This will only become a comfortable situation for the wife over time as the husband shows his consistency. As you both step into your appropriate roles, your marriage will take on a new light. What was once a burden will become easier because you are now working as you were designed to.

TAKING ACTION

Exercise 1.1   *Being a Godly Example*

In what area(s) do you need to focus on improving and aligning your personal life and relationship with what God prescribes for the sake of your marriage? for the sake of your children?

Exercise 1.2   *Letting Scripture Speak to You*

Read Song of Songs. What does it speak to you?

Exercise 1.3   *My Spiritual Leadership*

For the men, write a brief paragraph defining what your spiritual leadership looks like.

How did it go? Did you have difficulty writing down the spiritual elements you bring to the table in leading your wife and family?

Notes to Self—
What Is My Marriage Supposed to Look Like?

_____

_____

_____

_____

_____

_____

_____

_____

_____

_____

_____

_____

_____

_____

_____

_____

_____

_____

_____

_____

_____

_____

_____

_____

Chapter Two

Great Expectations

Sheila sits on the sofa tapping and rotating the pencil in her hand. Tap eraser, turn, tap lead and turn. Around the pencil goes as she twirls it between her fingers, the repetitive motion an unconscious emotional outlet. Her expression is serious as she talks on the telephone to her friend Claire from work. "It's just that he doesn't seem to care about what I say."

"Really? What does he do when you expect something of him? What does he say?"

"I guess he's pretty good about doing the things that I ask him." Sheila thinks for a moment and slowly lets her thoughts slip from her lips as she formulates them. "I just...I feel like I have to tell him everything. Is it the same with Tom? From the way you talk, it seems like he already knows what to do."

Claire laughs. "You make Tom sound like a puppy. Listen, Sheila, he didn't come trained. We've been working on how we talk to one another since early in our relationship. And no, a year and a half into our marriage, the training has not ended."

Sheila sighs dramatically. "Oh, great! When does it get better?"

"When I said 'training' I was not just talking about him. I had to change some things myself," Claire says.

"I hear what you're saying. I know it takes two to tango and all that stuff. But I'm sorry, there are just some things that should happen without me having to say anything. It's what he doesn't do that drives me crazy. If he gave two cents for how I feel he wouldn't be such a jerk. Are all guys just stupid?"

Claire tries to focus Sheila. "Okay, what isn't he doing?"

"I don't know, come on."

Claire again tries to make a point. "I can't even get you to be specific with me about what you're looking for, and I'm a woman. Does Mark even know what your expectations are?" She can hear the sigh at the other end of the line. "Don't expect him to know what you want if you don't."

Sheila pauses to gather herself. "So it's all me."

"I didn't say that. I just know that I can get very frustrated with Tom when he doesn't meet my needs. My responsibility is to tell him what those needs are."

There is silence on Sheila's end.

"You might want to spend some time thinking about what you expect from Mark. You want to give the guy a fighting chance, you know?"

"Mark is not as dumb as he acts," Sheila says bluntly. "He knows what I want and he knows what he should be doing. He just doesn't want to do it. I've got to go now. I'm going to be late for my class."

What expectations do you have for your marriage? We all have expectations: about our careers, our relationships, our families, our futures, you name it. It is important to know where we are heading so that we can benchmark our progress. And we should assess those expectations from time to time because otherwise they could derail our progress in life and relationships.

Are your expectations for your marriage heading you toward divorce court or marital bliss? Please note that if your expectations lean toward the negative, that will directly affect the way you behave toward your spouse. It will certainly minimize your ability to communicate positively in your relationship. A problem many couples have is that they build on the negatives in the relationship and over time simply stop looking for the good things in their spouse and their marriage. When we feel emotionally distraught, we often look for the things that will support our negative emotions—rather than things that will lift us up. We will discuss more on that topic a little later.

At this juncture it is important to focus on the positives in your marriage. You need to periodically identify what behaviors were occurring when things were better; in other words, *what was I doing differently?* Notice that your spouse is not being addressed here. There is good reason for that. One of the keys to a healthy relationship is that both parties take responsibility for their own behavior. I am more interested in you than your spouse at this point for the simple reason that you do not have the ability to change them, only yourself. If, however, you begin to take responsibility for your own behavior and focus on positive improvements, it certainly can affect the dynamics of the relationship.

Ponder the following scripture before you move to the next question. As you do, listen to what God has to tell you. This may take more than a few minutes because sometimes our own hurt prevents us from wanting to hear what God has to say in a given situation.

> Call to me and I will answer you and tell you great
> and unsearchable things you do not know.
>
> Jeremiah 33:3

What does this scripture speak to you?

ASSESSING EXPECTATIONS

Sometimes we have behaved a certain way for so long that we are not even aware we are doing it. Even if we can't see it, God can. Some common impediments to a fulfilling relationship may have developed over time, a byproduct of years of pain. These assumptions may also be a result of beliefs and lies about yourself, or marriage in general, stemming from your family of origin when growing up. They may involve control issues, where our own insecurity forces us to hold on tight to our mate, often to the point of strangling the love out of our relationship.

Remember, there should be freedom in love. The misconception that love should just happen ("If they loved me the behaviors would be effortless") is simply that: a misconception. Another is the old mindreading game of "If they really loved me they should know." Or how about "My spouse and I should be doing everything together. Our love should be enough. Why do we need others?" What about friends? What about God? Another common belief that trips us up is "If my mate doesn't tell me they love me on a continual basis, they must not." The real question is why do you need so much affirmation? Just something to consider. These are some examples of the thinking that goes into undermining marital relationships. Do any of these strike a chord with you?

When a spouse takes the responsibility for their mate's happiness problems are bound to arise. The flipside of that coin, and just as unreasonable, is the spouse who expects their mate to make them happy. This is an interesting but absolutely implausible belief founded in faulty thinking. First off, do you really have that much power, the power to make others happy? Some people believe so. Happiness as an attitude; it is a matter of personal choice. This is not to say that things won't happen to you that will make you unhappy, but that is situational and involves temporary setbacks. These tend to be short-term, and you don't live your life there.

Unfortunately, some people live their lives unhappily as a matter of choice. Your obligation is to honestly assess how much your behavior contributes to their unhappiness—things *you are* responsible for.

Secondly, a problem arises when we view our marriage through a filter of faulty beliefs that put our spouse in a "no win" situation. When we do not consider the validity of our beliefs, when we simply accept them as they are—without understanding they may come from dysfunctional roots—we leave ourselves open to taking things personally. When we operate in our default mode we tend to view all of life's events from only our own perspective (healthy or not), rather than challenge our beliefs or consider the perspective of others.

We stack the deck against our spouse when we take everything personally and expect our spouse to make us happy. It's not your spouse's job to make you happy! Consider that maybe there is a greater call that ultimately results in happiness, which we will discuss when we explore our emotions in a later chapter. Remember that your perception of the outward appearance can be skewed (just food for thought).

TRUE OR FALSE: SLEUTHING OUT YOUR BELIEFS

Think about your favorite Agatha Christie mystery movie. The apparent villain has been apprehended by the steadfast constable. The astute old lady, who has spent years reading detective magazines, has done a little research of her own. Turns out the chief inspector was a bit hasty in pointing the finger of guilt. Our elderly armchair detective has been less hasty. When all is said and done, and after our dear lady has presented the pieces of the puzzle to the reluctant and often frustrated chief inspector, he has no choice but to reconsider his stand. The real culprit is apprehended after, no doubt, an exciting confrontation with our amateur sleuth, guns a-blazing.

What is the point of my dramatic buildup? Ask yourself: what is going to be necessary to convict the criminal, the actual perpetrator of the crime? Evidence! Our objective is to challenge those beliefs that you have about your relationship and your spouse. Are they beneficial or destructive? If you believe them to be accurate, upon what evidence do you base them? If you have no evidence in support of a belief, why are you holding onto it? What might happen if you choose not to accept that belief?

Remember, it is okay to examine what you believe; in fact it is highly recommended. This is one way to address the lies that lead to faulty thinking. The continual gathering of evidence to support what you believe will only expose the lies or reinforce healthy beliefs, neither of which is a bad thing.

The bottom line regarding expectations is to be wary. In many cases if we rely on our expectations and they are unrealistic, or based on past events with no consideration toward the possibility for change, they can create a self-fulfilling prophecy. In other words, if you choose to believe that an outcome is likely, you can create the scenario for that very belief to come true.

Let's assume that Harry has a dreaded fear of authority figures because his father was very critical of him. He comes into work that morning and sees a note from his boss on his desk: "My office—11:30 am." Immediately the anxiety begins to build. *What could he possibly want? I don't think he really likes me. He never talks to me; why does he want to see me now?* And so the internal conversation goes.

By 11:30 Harry has built up such a scenario of assumptions in his head that he is ready to defend everything from what he had for breakfast to why he voted the way he did in the last election! Most likely he will walk into that office with a huge chip on his shoulder, ready to be defensive at the slightest provocation. Just before Harry opens his mouth, his boss acknowledges his efforts and apologizes that he hasn't mentioned it before and would like to show his appreciation by increasing Harry's salary for a job well done. If Harry had expressed what he had been feeling, his foot would have gone directly down his throat—and potentially a nice raise out the window.

REMOVE THE DIVORCE CARD

Realizing how much internal dialogue can affect our behavior, you can understand the importance of removing the "D" card from the options in your marital deck. Also note that just because Jesus condemns divorce, except in the case of adultery, does not imply that God can't perform miraculous restoration in a relationship even where infidelity has occurred. You will see in some of the following testimonies that in spite of adultery, God can bring healing to a broken marriage. Forgiveness and repentance can reign supreme. God has the absolute ability to heal the pain and restore such relationships. I have witnessed it time and time again. Understand, however, that a couple must want what God has to offer.

The point here is to make sure that divorce does not become an option for you without exhausting every possibility to make your relationship not just work but flourish. If the potential for divorce is always a viable option, you will increase the odds of that card being played. Assess your internal belief system and ask yourself the question: is it time to make some adjustments? An exercise concluding this chapter will investigate God's stance on divorce.

When our expectations for our marriage are unrealistic, a series of potholes will litter the matrimonial highway. We can easily lose sight of God's design for our marriage; we can forget all the qualities that first attracted us to our spouse; and we can forget just how special our mate really is. We can get so caught up in our differences (often the things we found endearing at first) and forget that our spouse's strengths offset our own weaknesses and vice versa.

We begin to focus on how our partner can be fixed rather than understanding how God created them different from us. We focus on our feelings rather than the practice of love.

When it was all said and done, the apostle Paul had one expectation: "I eagerly expect and hope that I will in no way be ashamed, but will have sufficient courage so that now as always Christ will be exalted in my body, whether by life or by death" (Philippians 1:20). Paul's expectation was that Christ always be honored.

TAKING ACTION

Exercise 2.1   Assessing Expectations

Go someplace where you can be alone, someplace comfortable and with no intrusions. You may complete the following exercise either here in the space provided or in a personal journal or notebook. You may choose to keep it in a private place, away from the eyes of invasive youngsters. You can use this journal for all the subsequent exercises and activities if you like. Sit for about fifteen minutes, silently. *Make a list of six expectations you have for the future of your marriage.*

Now that you have completed your list, go back and reread it. Do you find more negatives in your expectations list than positives?

Exercise 2.2   Assessing Behaviors

What current behavior(s) might you need to change to move the marriage back to a time when it was more fulfilling? Ask yourself what positive behaviors you did in the past that you are no longer doing.

Exercise 2.3   Are My Expectations Realistic?

Make a list of ten expectations you have for your spouse. Complete this on your own; this is not a collaborative effort at this point.

Once you have completed this list, take some quiet time with your mate and share your list. Allow them to share theirs. What was the result? Did your spouse think your expectations were realistic and achievable? Are you each willing to work toward meeting some of those expectations?

Exercise 2.4   Letting the Scriptures Speak to You

Pick up your Bible and write out the following scriptures. What do they speak to you regarding divorce?

Malachi 2:13-16
Genesis 2:24
Romans 7:1-3
1 Corinthians 7:10-16
Matthew 5:23-24
Matthew 5:31-32
Matthew 18:15-18

The intent of including these scriptures is not to compound any guilt or shame you may feel from a past divorce. The idea is to remove divorce as an option in your current relationship, forcing you to try other avenues of resolving your relationship issues.

Notes to Self—
Great Expectations

Chapter Three

The Cornerstone of a Healthy Marriage— Selfishness versus Selflessness

What causes fights and quarrels among you? Don't they come from your desires that battle within you? You want something but don't get it. You kill and covet, but you can't have what you want. You quarrel and fight. You do not have, because you do not ask God. When you ask, you do not receive, because you ask with wrong motives, that you may spend what you get on your pleasures.

James 4:1-3

A fruitful and healthy relationship is built on a fundamental cornerstone, defining the difference between selfishness and selflessness. We will spend some time over the next few pages exploring these two concepts that sound very similar but are at opposite ends of the contentment spectrum. Before we begin, however, let's take a moment to share.

THE DEVELOPMENT OF SELFISHNESS

Imagine a child about two years old, with no discernible expression on his face. He sits quietly in a corner watching the hustle and bustle of the room around him. Father comes into the room, looks at his watch, then sits on the couch. The child rises and moves toward his father, arms outstretched. The father suddenly remembers the task that needed to be completed before he rushed off to work. Up he bounces, moving quickly past the child.

The child's expression is distinctly noticeable now. His big brown eyes look sad as he lowers his arms and whimpers quietly. His eyes light up as he notices Mother, who has stepped out of the bedroom. His arms extend once more, craving a hug, some sort of affection from his mother. She stands by the couch and continues chatting on her cell phone. She proceeds down the hall into the darkness, as if not even noticing the child. The child's arms and head both lower. He drops to the floor and sits quietly. Can you imagine what the child is feeling at this moment?

Dad is very involved in his work, keeping food on the table and a roof over the family's head. Mother wants to do better, but Dad is so obsessed with his work that she has sole responsibility of the household, to say nothing of the fact that she too holds down a job. It's tough to make ends meet these days. In fact, Dad is so caught up in his work, spending time with his guy friends, and keeping up with the latest sports scores that Mom feels neglected. His lack of attention makes her feel unattractive.

As time goes by, Mother becomes more irritable and less interested in making the marriage a go. She certainly can't do it by herself. She can feel everything slowly slipping away. Some of her

downtime leads her to partake in a drink or two. This is a conve-
nient way of numbing the pain. The frequency of her drinking
increases as her disillusionment increases. Everyone is so caught
up in themselves that there doesn't seem to be much time for that
poor child. All he wants is some love and affection, the security of
someone who cares.

The family behaviors continue through the years. The little boy
continues to reach out to his parents for that love in a variety of
ways. Nothing seems to change for the long term so the child,
now ten, comes to accept his fate. He begins to close off. He stops
expecting. Many of you can feel for that child and understand his
plight. Some of you may be able to relate on a very personal level.

When children come into the world their primary emotional
need is the love and affection of their caregivers, their mother and
father. Unfortunately, all too often in my counseling career, when
sitting down with a young man, one scenario repeats itself. When
I ask "Did your father love you?" they look quizzical as they contemplate the question. "Well, sure. My dad always made sure that
we had a roof over our heads. Gosh, he worked all the time. I wish
he'd had more time to go to my baseball games, but he did what
he needed to do. We never went wanting. Yeah, it would have been
nice if he had been home more often, but, hey, what are you going
to do? You can't have everything, right?"

I repeat the question. "Take a minute, there is no rush to answer. I asked you if your dad loved you." The pause that occurs as
they contemplate the question for a second time is quite telling.
All too often the response cycle goes something like this. A look
of confusion, as if to wonder why I asked the question again. They
often look down for a moment. The message is sinking deeper. A
look of slight anger registers on their face; next comes sadness,
then the realization. Now they really understand the question.

I've gone through years of psychology classes. I understand the
theory. I know why counselors and therapists are told to maintain

a healthy distance from those they counsel—I get that. As the tears of realization flow from the eyes of the biggest, proudest, toughest guys you might imagine, I am not worried about containing myself. They need to understand that I understand, and more importantly that God understands. On many occasions I share in the grief and loss they experience in that moment of time—the moment they recognize that the need for love was never met. At which point my goal is to get them realigned with the Father who never ignored them, nor left them.

> For God so loved the world that he gave his one and only Son, that whoever believes in him shall not perish but have eternal life.
>
> John 3:16

What is evidenced in that scripture is this: God loves you and wants nothing more than to spend eternity with you!

Understand that there is no benefit to condemning our parents. In most cases parents do what they believe to be the right thing, based on their own knowledge. This knowledge often comes from how they were brought up, their own life experiences, and their own pain and insecurities. In fact, none of us is perfect, and none of us will parent perfectly. That is exactly why Jesus Christ had to come to this earth, to fill in the gap for our inadequacies. All the money, gifts, work ethic, keeping food on the table and a roof over our head will never substitute for the love, acceptance, and affection that a parent is supposed to demonstrate to their children. When these are the substitutes for godly love, damage is inevitable in our upbringing.

The scarring that often occurs throughout childhood and adolescence can contribute to many lies being created in our belief system. A common one is that God could never love us. If our parents are to be an earthly example of who God is to us, and they don't fulfill their obligation, it's easy to understand how this can occur. This certainly has a profound effect on our spiritual relationship.

The child learns early on that this inherent need for love will go unmet, based on what has been demonstrated to him. In short order, the child begins to withdraw and shut down, not expecting the return of love and affection. He learns not to need it. This behavior is a reasonable response if you think about it. How many times does a person expose their vulnerability and have it rejected before they begin to withhold it altogether? They will only be hurt a certain number of times before they stop putting themselves in that hurtful situation. Now we have a child who has learned not to need love from others, and he becomes self-sufficient, depending on himself for his needs to be met and never extending himself to others.

This same child grows up, twenty years old, loaded with self-sufficiency. Now a young man, he continues to believe that the world functions based on his views of it—views established by areas in which his upbringing was lacking. People cannot be trusted. It is dangerous and painful to share feelings. Vulnerability is a prescription for heartache. He refuses to practice transparency or let others into the innermost parts of his being. Essentially he is thinking very egocentrically and everything revolves around his own perception. In essence his youthful self-sufficiency has become adult selfishness. How do you think this dynamic can affect a marital relationship? How might it be affecting yours?

ADDRESSING OUR OWN SELFISHNESS

After identifying areas in which we may be exhibiting selfish behaviors, what can we do about it? How can we change our selfishness?

1. Present yourself to God; ask him to make you aware of your own selfishness. Be prepared: if you ask God to show you, he will be faithful. Your job is to be ready to receive it.

2. Meditate and internalize the following scriptures:

    Greater love has no one than this, that he lay down his life for his friends.

    John 15:13

    Nobody should seek his own good, but the good of others.

    1 Corinthians 10:24

3. Try doing the opposite of what you feel. It sounds unusual but consider that your autopilot may currently be guided by your hurt (not the best compass), so your natural tendency is to self-protect that hurt. Take a chance and see what happens. We can only update our script by taking chances and gathering new evidence to see if our childhood beliefs are still accurate. Have these childhood beliefs skewed our adult perception of relationships, of life? Challenge your adult perceptions. Are they accurate?

Remember, in spite of what happened in your childhood, regardless of the pain that may have been inflicted, intentionally or unintentionally, you are no longer that child. You are an adult and bear the consequences of your adult actions. Ask yourself, "What am I going to do about it?" It's time to take responsibility for your own behavior. Seek God's strength and help as you begin to take responsibility for the one thing that you can control: your own behavior.

In spite of the hurt and frustration you may be feeling, depending on the current state of your marriage, it is important to begin taking responsibility for your own behavior and the decisions that you make. After all, who pays the consequences of your actions? Ultimately you do and perhaps your children.

I would like to present to you the testimony of a couple who were nearly destroyed by selfishness. It is important to remember that the dynamics in a relationship are seldom, if ever, one-sided. Selfishness will cast a spell of justification on almost any behavior if you don't filter your behaviors through God. As you read this testimony keep in mind that the plain text is the husband's story and the italicized text represents his wife's perspective of the same events.

IN THEIR OWN WORDS: THE HIGH COST OF SELFISHNESS

In my early teens I decided to pave my own path, a path of destruction. I was partying and doing all the things that came with it, throwing responsibility to the wind. No surprise, I became a young mother.

I met my future husband while I was attending college. He was such a gentle spirit; he had long hair and played in a band. He was funny and we always had a great time, but I always knew that he wanted more than just friendship. Over time the emotional attraction grew stronger, and before you knew it we were living together.

The unfortunate circumstances of my childhood contributed to the type of husband and father I would become. My mother divorced my paternal father when I was two or three years old, and she remarried about a year later to a man whom she met one month prior to their marriage. Throughout my childhood, my parents' love for one another was demonstrated by simple greeting cards during the holidays and on their anniversaries. That was the extent of it. My childhood was littered with a variety of other damage including alcoholism, domestic violence, and sexual abuse. When the time came to start my own family, I swore that I would never physically abuse my wife or children and never abandon them. I took pride in fulfilling my "role" as provider. Unfortunately I didn't have much of a model to base it on. As it turns out, I was a great student of the self-centeredness I saw displayed in my upbringing.

We married in May. Our first few years of marriage were bliss. I had given up the life I had been living years before. However, financially it started to get tight. We decided that it was time for me to go back to work and get a part-time job right after our son turned a year old. My husband thought it would be best that he also pick up a second job. It was then that our marriage took a turn.

I learned later that this second job, working in a machine shop, provided a party-time environment. He played his bass, partied, drank, and they were all paid to kick back and have a good time. I sat home many a night thinking what a wonderful husband he was to want to take care of his family, not knowing the truth. This was a precursor for what was to come.

At my suggestion we began attending a Bible study. I thought it would help us because some cracks were starting to show in our relationship. It was in this study that his view about God started to change and we ventured out to find a church.

While in our new church, he decided to quit his job at the machine shop. I believe he was becoming convicted by his behavior while at work. I may not have known what he was doing, but God did! He tried out for the church's recovery ministry band; he became the bass player. I was thrilled because he was a recovering alcoholic, and I thought this would draw him closer to the Lord.

The ministry had a testimony night and asked my husband to give his. I sat so eager and excited to hear his testimony. It was there that night that I learned what he had been doing at his second job. My blood ran cold and I was in complete shock. He had been lying to me all along.

Next, he quit his longtime employment and decided to take a supervisor position out in Costa Mesa, California. He worked long hours and weekends. The kids and I didn't see him much. I took care of everything because he simply didn't have time. I started to feel lonely, and the resentment grew. We started to move in different directions, and things seemed to be falling apart.

My marriage was starting to feel more like an obligation to my children than a loving relationship with my wife. The feelings for my wife were dying. Although I had accepted Jesus into my life, I was not serving him because I did not love my wife in a way that was pleasing to him. Rather than focusing on my wife and marriage, I focused more on myself.

I started to notice that he was getting calls in the wee hours of the morning. We started to argue more, and trust started to become an issue. A short time later my father-in-law passed away, and some of his employees showed up at the memorial service to offer support. I remember it like it was yesterday. Standing before me was a woman, older than I. As she and I made eye contact I recall her looking at me as a woman in competition. It struck me as odd, but something deep inside of me began to suspect her intentions.

It wasn't apparent to me that I was not nurturing my marriage, because I felt I was doing all that was expected as a husband, certainly based on the model I was raised with. I was placing my job before the needs of my wife, and I made it very clear that I expected her to be just as independent. What I was attributing to independence was really selfishness, plain and simple. What I was telling my wife through my words and actions was that she was on her own. As I became more engrossed with my job, my wife realized she could not depend on me as a married partner; we grew to become married singles. As I became more of a stranger in my home, without affection from my spouse, I sought validation through my job and my co-workers.

We argued daily when we did see each other. He stopped wearing his wedding ring. We were not intimate, and I noticed he would look at me weird when he would come home. All the signs were there, but I still wanted to give him the benefit of the doubt. I would confront him on numerous occasions. He would say, "There's nothing going on. You're crazy!" and I believed him.

Finally I had made my mind up to leave my husband. Our arguments were getting volatile, and I had a complete lack of trust and respect for him. He started to feel the heat and the pressure to leave. It disgusted me to even look at him. I stopped going to church. I am a strong woman and knew I could make it on my own. I wasn't the first woman to do it on her own, and I wouldn't be the last.

While at the job, I was viewed as a strong leader with a great work ethic, and I received high praise from upper management. That validation was confirmed as I received promotions and assumed greater responsibilities. I foolishly believed that I was meeting all the needs of my family and that my wife should not have anything to complain about. Our marriage devolved to become one that was similar to what I saw growing up. I felt justified to have my own physical and emotional needs met by someone else since I wasn't feeling the love at home. By becoming involved with another woman at the workplace, I selfishly allowed my own dysfunction to override what was right.

I received a phone call from some man. He said to me, "My wife and your husband are having an affair!" I felt flushed. I knew it! She was the one I suspected all along. I was perplexed about what to do. I was so angry. So I waited for him to come home. Once again he lied and once again I believed him. I recall praying and asking God to draw me close to my husband. I didn't know why but I knew I had to. I made the decision to truly and wholeheartedly serve the Lord. Shortly after that prayer and during our marriage group my husband revealed to me that he had indeed had an "emotional affair" with that woman. I was so heartbroken and devastated. Days were dark for me, and I relied on my faith to pull us through. On some of those days I still felt like he wasn't being truthful and forthcoming about that affair.

Once my sins came to light, I lied to my wife and denied that I had sex with this other woman and that it was more about meeting for coffee and talking. Because I would not be completely honest to my wife, and myself, we never received the full healing in our marriage.

My walk with the Lord grew stronger and deeper. Soon I found out we were expecting our fourth child. Our oldest was already twenty, our second oldest was fifteen, and our youngest son was eight. I was told I could never have any more children. I was in complete shock. But you see, God is so good and he is so faithful. He knew what we would need in our lives. The dynamics of our family were shot and dysfunctional and barely getting on the right track. I really felt my faith being put to the test. The pregnancy became a high-risk one and required me to be put on bed rest for the duration of my pregnancy. I was down for four and a half months. I was told to abort, but I refused and handed it over to God. I felt that the Lord wanted to bind us together and move forward in our marriage, leaving the affair behind. It was time to forgive, but every so often something was still nagging at me even during my pregnancy. We gave birth to a beautiful baby girl early the next year. I found myself praying and praying to God, asking him to draw me closer to my husband.

My wife became pregnant, and the whole episode with my affair became an afterthought while we prepared for another child. Because we did not fully address the issues we had with our relationship, I became caught up in the same cycle of not feeling loved, respected, and appreciated. All of my wife's attention seemed to be focused on the baby. It wasn't long before I started to seek respect and appreciation from yet another woman.

My actions told my wife that I had abandoned our sacred bond, that my pride and ego were more important than her and our children's needs. My behavior proved her to be right. Though I had accepted Jesus as my Savior, I was oblivious to my sins because I did not nurture my relationship with the Lord. Instead of cleaving to my wife, I fell to the temptations of my flesh. Conviction wasn't an issue for me because I was far from his voice.

I'm not a woman to go through my husband's things, but as clear as can be, I heard a voice tell me to pick up his cell phone one evening. Lo and behold, I found a text from a woman saying that she was sorry she could not get his call. It was odd the text was under his boss's name.

I immediately took it to him. His expression gave it away and I knew it was another woman. What a fool I was! Again, I'm left with the pain and hurt of having to face some serious decisions. The night erupted into a physical altercation. My life was now in a place where I could no longer hide my husband's sins from our older girls. I had to make decisions. What would I tell our son?

I explained that I could not live in a marriage where we were not evenly yoked. My husband needed to understand that I would not tolerate any more of his lies, and I decided it was best for him to leave.

There were many sleepless nights. I prayed and asked the Lord in the midst of my anguish to please watch over my husband, to heal his heart. One night as I was sleeping, the Lord woke me up. Very clearly he told me, "Bring your husband home and grieve your marriage together. You will mourn your marriage, but I promise I will make you whole and new again!" The tears were streaming down my face. He also told me to pick up the Bible and open it; amazingly it went right to 1 Peter 4:12, "Dear friends, do not be surprised at the painful trial you are suffering, as though something strange were happening to you. But rejoice that you participate in the sufferings of Christ, so that you may be overjoyed when his glory is revealed." Although I was in a place of hurt and fear, I knew that my God would keep me covered. He would give me the strength I needed to carry on. I came to recognize that I too had made some damaging contributions to our marriage. The Lord used this opportunity to show me who I was and who I wasn't in him.

The Lord had begun a transformation in my wife when she drew closer to God and put him at the head of everything. Without this rededication in her life, my wife would never have considered reconciliation of our marriage a possibility. I can't even imagine the hurt and pain that she has felt because of my choices. We separated for a brief period of time, and I had to deal with the consequences of what I had done in order to get my life back on track. She could have allowed the pain that I had caused to permanently harden her heart against me, but instead the Lord spoke to her and told her to have me come back home to start the healing. It was not just about my coming back home, it was about us starting to deal with the issues in our marriage that drove us apart.

My husband came home and we cried for many nights. We began the process of getting to know one another. We both realized that it would be a lengthy process and God's forgiveness needed to be the foundation if we were going to move forward.

My husband was not being transparent so God exposed his lies, and he also exposed things that I needed to begin to address in my own life. I know now that had I known the truth about my husband some years ago, I would have left him and I would have never known God the way I do now.

My wife's desire to please the Lord and forgive me has allowed us to rebuild our marriage on a solid foundation. Her choice showed me how much she loved me in a way that words never could. It wasn't until the Lord brought my sins to light and put me in a place to receive His love, through friends and church family, that I gained a clear understanding of my role as a husband and father that serves God. I continue to offer restitution to my wife for as long as the healing and reestablishing trust will take, as it is an unfortunate consequence of my actions. We have been restored through our trust in the Lord.

Today we love each other so much, and with each touch and expression of love the memories of the hurt fade. Side by side, our passion is to reach out to others to tell them who God is and his design for marriage. Being steadfast in his Word and never wavering in faith, we let the Lord lead the way saying, "all for the glory and praise to God!"

SELFLESSNESS IS ESSENTIAL

In a marriage it is essential to develop an attitude of selflessness. Let's take a few moments and think about the state of your current relationship. It's easy to say that the entire problem is the other person's fault. Perhaps your spouse has done some things that have hurt you very deeply. You are two different people and you are bound to do things that ruffle one another's feathers. Fact is, it takes two people to make or break a marriage. It's an issue of dynamics. I want you to meditate before the Lord and be honest. Ask Him to show you the areas in which you have helped to create or facilitate the current dynamics of your marriage. At the conclusion of this chapter you will be asked to complete a personal contribution list. This will be a demonstration of taking responsibility for your part in moving the relationship in the direction it is currently. Taking responsibility is a major step toward change and healing.

TAKING ACTION

Exercise 3.1   Problematic Issues in My Marriage

Briefly describe the four issues you would consider to be the most problematic in your marriage.

Now let's take another look at this list. Look at it in light of what has been shared about the development of selfishness throughout this chapter. This is an opportunity for both you and your spouse to take an honest look at yourselves and take responsibility. Of the four items that you have listed, how many of them are a byproduct of your own selfishness? Place a red "X" in front of the ones that are. Remember that selfishness could be a result of hurt you have felt over the years, current marital dynamics, lies that you believe, consequences of your refusing to be vulnerable, or having made the decision to retire to your corner of the boxing ring and not change. There can be any number of reasons. Think about it and be honest with yourself because those closest to you probably already know, and you certainly aren't fooling God. Ask God to reveal the truth to you. Give yourself some time to process this information, then sit down with your mate and share your conclusions.

Exercise 3.2   *Assessing the Accuracy of Our Adult Perceptions*

What action steps are you and your spouse going to take individually or together to assess your adult perceptions and realign them with the truth? Jot down a few things that come to mind. In other words, how will you challenge the lies that you believe. It may be very helpful to seek out your closest friends and ask them if they see you in the same way that you see yourself.

Exercise 3.3   *My Contribution List*

Make a list of your personal contributions that have created the state in which the marriage currently exists. This is a time for honesty and transparency. Ask God to show you those things of which you are not aware. Take this assignment very seriously. Set aside the alone time necessary to complete it. Eliminate outside distractions as much as possible. Be thorough. This list is for you; do not show it to your mate, but do not lose it since we will come back to it at a later date.

Notes to Self—
Selfishness versus Selflessness

Chapter Four

Have You Lost
That Loving Feeling?—
Feelings and Behavior

The sky is gray and the wind blows through the trees on this blustery afternoon. The usual children are not playing in the neighborhood. Perhaps some are still in school while others are anticipating the coming storm. The rain begins to gently tap the pavement. The flowers in the bed sway back and forth with the weight of the raindrops. Peering through the dining room picture window is a woman. Her left elbow rests on the dining room table while her hand rests on her chin and cheek. She sits quietly gazing out the window as she puts together her thoughts. Sheila, half lost in the hypnotic cadence of the raindrops, refocuses on the task at hand. She picks up her pen and slides her journal dead center. With what appears to be reluctance or perhaps futility, she puts pen to paper.

Well, it's me again. I had hoped to express some startling revelation. Not today. Mark seems to be growing more distant. I know it's not all his fault, even though I don't like to admit it. What is happening to us? Things used to be so different. I always felt like we had a strong bond. I remember all the sweet things he used to do for me, the things he used to say. Even though it seems to be getting more difficult, I know I still love him. Why do I let his behavior make me so crazy? Why does he do the things that drive me crazy? He must know how much they hurt me. Is that why he does them? I don't know. What can I do to get through to him? I can feel my love for him slowly beginning to seep from me. I know that it's not right! It's just so frustrating. If he doesn't begin to change, begin to do something about it, I'm afraid where it will all lead to. Was our marriage a mistake? Help me with the answer! What am I supposed to do? How am I supposed to behave? I just don't like the person that I am becoming. I don't like the person that he is making me. I hope, I truly hope that I can get that love, that feeling for Mark back. We've been through so much. I just don't feel like there is anything that I can do. Lord, help me do the right thing. I don't feel like doing anything!

If selflessness is the cornerstone of a healthy marriage, understanding our emotions and the effect they have on our relationship is the mortar. First, consider the concept of feelings. Merriam-Webster defines feelings this way: "an emotional state or reaction." Oftentimes feelings are a response elicited by a circumstance or situation. Now let's pose a question. In your opinion, are feelings good or bad? Why? In the pages that follow we will address this question and discover just where your feelings belong in the scope of what occurs to you during the course of the day. Understanding how feelings affect you, and the relationships around you, can have an important impact on the decisions you make. It's essential to realize that what you may feel can determine outcomes in a variety of ways.

ROMANCE AND REALITY

The idea of romantic love has been expressed in an infinite number of venues. When speaking of romantic love I am not talking about *being* romantic in your relationship; these are two different things. Let's differentiate. Shakespeare's *Romeo and Juliet* is a great literary example of two star-crossed lovers whose family feuding prevents them from being together, leading to their ultimate ends. This is wonderfully romantic stuff. The movies are obsessed with the idea of romantic love and that our love for one another will conquer any adversity.

During dating and courtship, it is hard to find any flaws in the "most beautiful person on the face of this planet." Well, we tend to ignore the flaws. It's the whole "rose-colored glasses" syndrome. Romantic love certainly has a place in the development of relationships. *But there are two things to remember about romantic love. First, it tends not to be very realistic.* Romantic love typically does not allow for imperfections. This is not to say that people in romantic love are perfect, it's just that many times neither party is willing to assess or address imperfections in the other person. We allow the relationship to run the course, believing (unrealistically) that things will get better in time. They don't get better, and they often get much worse as your mate becomes more comfortable with you. However, since you never addressed the issue to begin with, they are baffled by your frustration with the behavior now. After all, they have been consistent.

A benign example may be that your spouse is always late to engagements. It bothers you, but you never say anything about it. You might be afraid they will consider you controlling if you share this gripe. Years later, now married and the issue never addressed, they continue to be late. It doesn't matter whether the appointment is important or no big deal. You are becoming more aware that the tardiness reflects on you as well. On the next appointment, you explode all over your spouse, sharing the years of frustration you've experienced with what you consider a total lack of respect on their part. They stare at you, befuddled by your emotional outburst.

The second thing to remember about romantic love is that it is short-term. As we settle into our relationships or marriage, we start to see the other person in all their glory, warts and all. Since many of the red flags that you were willing to ignore while you were dating are becoming more prevalent, you get increasingly angry because things simply don't get better over time without putting forth an effort to make them better.

FEELINGS: GOOD OR BAD?

The most common response to this question is that overall they are a good thing. The feelings themselves may not always be good (anger, frustration, sadness), but in general they are a good thing. Certainly, when Jesus came to earth in human form, his emotions and feelings were on display. Jesus demonstrated righteous anger when the sellers were ripping off those who came to worship by charging exorbitant amounts of money to purchase the required animal sacrifices. Jesus went so far in his anger as to turn over the sacrifice tables, making them fully aware of his displeasure.

We see demonstrations of sadness and depression in the Garden of Gethsemane as Jesus agonizes over his fate. In Mark 14:34, Jesus clearly makes his feelings known: "My soul is overwhelmed with sorrow to the point of death," he tells Peter, James, and John. He asks them to keep watch while he goes up a little farther to pray. Upon his return he finds them sleeping. "Are you asleep? Could you not keep watch for one hour?" Jesus shows obvious disappointment with the three disciples. There are also times of happiness recorded in the life of Jesus. If feelings are good enough for Jesus, they are good enough for me.

Whether feelings are good or bad is not really the issue. We obviously have feelings. Some of those feelings are good, while others are not so good. The core issue is not the feelings themselves. The important thing to consider is the consequences of those feelings. In other words, what do we do with our feelings? How are they demonstrated in our behavior?

We will refer once again to the expert, Merriam-Webster. Behavior is defined as "the manner of conducting oneself; anything that an organism does involving action and response to stimulation; the response of an individual, group, or species to its environment." This is where the problem often unfolds. Events happen to us throughout the course of our day that trigger an emotional response. Often that emotional response leads to a behavior tied to that response. In other words, we determine our behavior based on what we feel about that particular person, circumstance, or event.

A common example: you are driving along the freeway. Suddenly a car comes off the on-ramp merging onto the freeway. They merge right in front of you, forcing you to swerve into the next lane nearly causing an accident. You have experienced surprise, fear, and anger almost simultaneously. Taking the personal assault angrily, you pull up alongside them and offer the all too common single-finger gesture of dissatisfaction at the behavior of others. You know nothing about that other person. A variety of reasons may have caused that reaction from the other person. Reasons that have nothing to do with you personally. Scripture is very clear:

> We demolish arguments and every pretension that sets itself up against the knowledge of God, and we take captive every thought to make it obedient to Christ.
>
> 2 Corinthians 10:5

We are called to live intentionally. If that were not the case, why would God have left us the Holy Bible as a love letter from Him and clear instruction on how we should live our lives?

Here lies the problem. How often do you allow your feelings to dictate your behavior? How many times do you do what your feelings tell you to do? The curious thing about feelings is that it is sometimes difficult to determine what truly triggered a particular feeling that just swept over us. Spend the next week participating in the following exercise.

IDENTIFYING OUR EMOTIONS

This exercise can be a very effective part of becoming aware and controlling your feelings from here on out. Whenever you feel a negative emotion overcome you—anger, sadness, anxiety, or any other—grab your journal or notebook. Write the day's date on the left side of the page. On the right side of the page, jot down the feeling that has overcome you. Next, think back to a few moments ago and ask yourself this question: "What event or situation just occurred that triggered that emotion?" Jot that down on the next couple of lines. Ask yourself, "Is the emotion I am feeling appropriate to the situation that triggered it?" Finally, offer an alternative or two to your assessment of the situation—an assessment that does not revolve around your perspective (Figure 4.1).

In many instances, if you are honest, you will find that the emotional response is far more intense than the situation warrants. Try it over the next week and see what you discover. Often what has occurred is more related to taking things personally rather than a justified emotional response. This is why it is dangerous to allow our emotions to dictate our behavior.

Example:
Date: *Monday, November 15th*

Feeling	Situation	Reasonable?
Angry	*Aunt Harriet didn't ask me to*	*No*
Frustrated	*make my famous deviled eggs*	
	for Thanksgiving. They are	
	wonderful and everyone loves them.	
	She asked me to bring the rolls.	
	She hates for me to get any attention.	
	She is so insecure!	
Alternative	*Maybe Aunt Harriet just didn't think*	
	about my eggs; maybe she simply forgot.	
	I guess I could always ask her if she	
	would like for me to bring them.	
	I'll bring the rolls too.	

(Figure 4.1)

Let's use another driving example. Visualize this: you are driving down the freeway in your car. It has been months since you washed it. The windshield is filthy. It has rained a few times, just enough to muddy the filth on the window. There are bird droppings everywhere, making it very difficult to see. That doggone cat that your neighbor feeds is constantly climbing all over the hood and windshield, leaving its grimy paw prints everywhere.

You get the picture. Your ability to see clearly while you drive down the freeway will be considerably impaired. Our mind is sometimes like that. During the course of our lives a variety of things contribute to what we believe about life and ourselves. The way we were raised by our parents is a contributing factor, and our religious beliefs certainly impact how we think. The negative messages we receive on our journey through life affect us. The expectations others place on us can impact as well. If we don't assess the validity of all these beliefs and release the negative ones, our windshield (or filter) can get very dirty, affecting how we receive information. All the gunk from the past impacts how we perceive what is going on in the present. Some of what we believe about ourselves can be simply inaccurate. Can you see how our acceptance of these internal lies can affect our feelings, having a direct impact on our behavior if we simply choose to stay in autopilot? This concept directly impacts our ability to communicate with our spouse and with others.

Thoughts and feelings are directly related, and it is important to monitor our thoughts, filtering them through what Scripture teaches. So what about behavior? Let's look again at Mark 14 when Jesus is describing how he feels about the upcoming events and the sacrifice he will make on the cross. He describes his emotional state as "overwhelmed with sorrow to the point of death" (v. 34). When he separates himself from his three disciples, he falls to his knees and prays, "Abba, Father, everything is possible for you. Take this cup from me. Yet not what I will, but what you will" (v. 36).

What we see here is a demonstration of a man with feeling. The feelings are real, honest, and easy to validate. The resulting action is the important thing to consider here. In his crying out, in no way was Jesus trying to wiggle free of his obligation. He didn't choose to avoid the cross even though his feelings might have told him that would be best, certainly easier. No, Jesus' behavior was consistent to what he knew was God's will.

LOVE AS DEFINED BY OUR CREATOR

Let's take a journey down memory lane. In all likelihood, the following scripture was recited at your own wedding. Let's revisit it.

Love is patient, love is kind. It does not envy, it does not boast, it is not proud. It is not rude, it is not self-seeking, it is not easily angered, it keeps no record of wrongs. Love does not delight in evil but rejoices with the truth. It always protects, always trusts, always hopes, always perseveres.

1 Corinthians 13:4-8

Do you notice anything unusual about this passage of scripture? Note that it is all action driven, contrary to what our society would have you believe. Lasting love is not emotionally fueled, although feelings are certainly produced. What this tells me is that a healthy, long-lasting and loving relationship is based on my desire to put forth the necessary efforts to keep it healthy. I do not determine my effort by what I feel like doing.

Bill comes home after a grueling day at the office; nothing came off as planned. His head wouldn't stop pounding. His computer was being its normal stubborn self. The traffic on the way home was horrendous. In general, Bill feels lousy. He pulls into the driveway and walks up to the front door. Now Bill has a decision to make. He has a choice. He can walk through the front door and meet his family behaving exactly how he feels—cranky, agitated, and aggressive, dumping that anger on his wife.

How do you think that delightful presentation will be received? She will shoot back with both barrels, taking all of Bill's behaviors in a personal way. After all, she is the new target of his aggression. What alternative does she have? He attacked her. That just makes Bill angrier, so he escalates the confrontation. His voice increases in volume, and maybe he throws down his briefcase for dramatic effect. Offended, she comes right back at him. So the conflict escalates right up the scale! Bill's feelings dictated his behavior, to his disadvantage, and the unfortunate recipients were his family.

Here's an alternative scenario. Bill stands at the door, feeling lousy but aware of it. He decides that regardless of how he feels, he is going to demonstrate love and affection toward his wife and family. Bill enters his home and gives his wife a kiss and tells her how much he loves her. How do you think that reception will be met? If she is monitoring her behavior (maybe she had a rough day with the kids, etc.) the odds are great that she will respond to her husband's loving display and reciprocate. That will affect Bill's emotional state in a positive fashion, actually reducing some of the aggression. Then he reciprocates and back and forth it goes. Bill begins to feel those negative emotions dissipate.

You might say to yourself, *that's just being fake!* No, it is you doing what is right by your spouse, which in the end has the potential for great benefit for you. Do you enjoy conflict in your relationship? Keeping your feelings in check is a very practical way of facilitating that goal.

> But the wisdom that comes from heaven is first of
> all pure; then peace-loving, considerate, submissive,
> full of mercy and good fruit, impartial and sincere.
> Peacemakers who sow in peace raise a harvest of
> righteousness.
>
> James 3:17-18

Being aware of your emotional state and choosing your behaviors is one method to restore some peace in the relationship. Some of the other methods include the following.

Don't make happiness (a feeling) the ultimate goal in your marriage. It sounds contrary to what you hear; everyone says, "I just want to be happy in my marriage." Your desire should be to seek that deeper contentment known as joy. Emotionally we can be like a rollercoaster depending on what the day might bring. Happiness tends not to be consistent whereas the deeper sense of contentment or satisfaction (joy) remains constant regardless of what's going on around us. True contentment is based on selflessness with a distinct priority system made up of three priorities.

1. *Model Christ in your life and in your relationships.* The example Jesus sets in Scripture is the one we should follow while interacting with others. Christ's example is demonstrated in the following passage:

> If you have any encouragement from being united with Christ, if any comfort from love, if any fellowship with the Spirit, if any tenderness and compassion, then make my joy complete by being like-minded, having the same love, being one in spirit and purpose. Do nothing out of selfish ambition or vain conceit, but in humility consider others better than yourselves. Each of you should look not only to your own interests, but to the interests of others. Your attitude should be the same as that of Christ Jesus...
>
> Philippians 2:1-5

2. *Focus on other people.* If you take the focus off yourself and spend more time focusing on others, you make it less likely that your motivations will be driven by your own selfish desires. This is not to say you should neglect yourself, because you can only pour into others if you stay emotionally, physically, and spiritually full. You simply do not become the priority as we shall see shortly.

> Nobody should seek his own good, but the good of others.
>
> 1 Corinthians 10:24

The therapeutic effect of stepping out of your own emotional state to serve others is amazing. Mary was diagnosed with cancer. Her knee-jerk reaction was to withdraw from the world. She lived in fear that any exposure to the outdoors, to the sun, would accelerate the cancer. Mary locked herself away, covering all the windows and never taking a step out of the house. She withdrew from other people, embarrassed by the hair loss associated with chemotherapy. She stopped coming to church, essentially stopped living.

What Mary had chosen to do is eliminate any new input or thought that would challenge her emotions. She simply recycled all the negative fear messages through her head. Her behavior followed suit and was dictated by those emotions. After consultation, she began challenging the fears and weighing the possible consequences of stepping outside her home. Commonly, we assume that things will be much worse than they actually end up being. One thing appeared certain: if Mary didn't take a chance, her fear would eat her alive.

The following week she came to church. The outpouring of love and acceptance was heartwarming and had a great impact on her. Having all these people walking alongside her gave Mary a new lease on life. Her hair grew back following the chemo treatments, and her joy and confidence returned even faster. This dear lady made the decision not to follow her feelings but choose her own behavior, in spite of those destructive feelings.

3. *Focus on yourself.* It's amazing how when you initiate the first two priorities, the attitude about the third changes drastically. When you demonstrate Christ and put others first, what you get back in the contentment of joy carries you through most of your other trials. Joy is the confident assurance and trust of God in our lives. Throughout his letter to the Philippians, Paul explains how his joy carried him through some pretty intense tribulation. Read through Philippians and discover for yourself the difference between happiness and joy.

Do what is "right" and let the appropriate emotions follow the

behavior. It's exciting to see how the confidence and security of right actions affect our emotional state. I always refer to the Bible in determining that "right" position. In the example given earlier, Bill comes home to his wife and family after a rough day of work. In choosing to do what is right and behave in a loving fashion, he has a direct effect on his emotional state simply because of what was reciprocated by his wife and family.

Live intentionally. As I stated in the introduction, the Scriptures are a guidebook to life, written by the one who created us. You benefit by living with intention and making decisions that guide the path of your life, with God's direction, rather than living haphazardly, just letting life happen to you.

Understand that none of us is perfect, not by a long shot! But if we make selflessness our goal rather than serving our own self-interest, the odds of receiving God's best in our lives increases tremendously.

In closing this section I would like to leave you with a practical technique that has been helpful for many. Remember, the issue is to focus more on our behavior rather than our emotions, certainly with regard to how we respond in our marriages. The term *mantra* refers to a word or phrase that is repeated often expressing an important belief. Let's look at one that will increase your awareness of your behavior, one that will affect the way you interact with your spouse.

How Will My Behavior Affect My Spouse?

Repeating this phrase mentally will help you think about what you are about to do or say. Rather than respond from our emotions, we can stop and really think about what we are about to say. Put this new mantra on sticky notes in places you frequent such as the bathroom mirror, the refrigerator, your dashboard, or wherever. Ingrain it into your thought processes so that it becomes your new autopilot. See how this simple effort affects the way you behave with your mate. The term *spouse* may be switched out with the name of anyone you have to deal with on a regular basis where you notice that your behavior has taken a negative turn. Your boss, your in-laws, your friend…use the mantra with anyone it might apply to. Monitoring your behavior will only work to your benefit and allow you to gain greater control of how you interact with other people.

TAKING ACTION

Exercise: 4.1   Assessing My Emotional Response

In the section "Identifying Our Emotions" you were shown how to journal your emotional responses by identifying your feeling(s), describing the situation that had just elicited that feeling(s), and assessing how reasonable your emotional response was to that event. You were then asked to identify alternative(s) that do not revolve around your perspective of the situation. Review the section if necessary. Over the next week, use this technique when you feel emotional responses surfacing. Jot down the results of using this technique. Are you finding that you take things too personally?

Exercise 4.2   Choosing My Behaviors

The next time you and your spouse come together, examine your emotional state. If you are feeling negative, make a decision about it. Decide to do what is right and greet your spouse in a positive fashion. Demonstrate loving behavior rather than the aggression you may be feeling. The first time you do this, jot down the results. How did your husband/wife respond to your positive greeting? How did your behavior impact your negative feelings?

Notes to Self—
Feelings and Behavior

_____

_____

_____

_____

_____

_____

_____

_____

_____

_____

_____

_____

_____

_____

_____

_____

_____

_____

_____

_____

_____

_____

_____

_____

Chapter Five

Forgiveness, Ugh!

Mark and Tom, Claire's husband, are spending their ritual Tuesday evening at the gym doing their sets. Mark is obviously lost in his thoughts. He hasn't said two words to Tom in the last twenty minutes.

Tom wipes the sweat from his brow. "Okay, buddy. What's up?"

Mark snaps out of it but is a bit reluctant to share. "Nothing, just thinking."

Tom laughs. "Really? Thanks for that great insight. You don't have to talk if you're not ready. Just know that if you want to talk, I'm here for you."

Mark smiles. "The five years that we've known you and Claire have been great. It's like we've known you guys forever. I've told you more in the past year than I've shared with anyone my entire life. It means a lot to me; trust doesn't come easy."

Tom nods understandingly. "I know."

"I love Sheila, I do. Sometimes it's so hard. It seems like we keep doing the same wrong things over and over. Like last month when I asked her to mail the mortgage payment and she forgot. I go nuts when the bills aren't paid on time! She knows that."

"And how late was the payment?"

Mark shakes his head. "It was three days before she finally got it sent out."

"When did it get to your mortgage company?"

Mark's tone is sarcastic. "Not until the fifth!"

"So it's due the first and it got there the fifth? So it got there in plenty of time? You guys weren't even near the end of the grace period, huh?" Tom smirks.

"That's not the point."

"It's exactly the point. Even your mortgage company extends grace. You act like this was some kind of epic disaster. Do you think she did it on purpose? I hope this wasn't your best example. Listen to your tone. So you've been holding onto this for a month? What do you do with the serious stuff?"

Mark is not thrilled with the way Tom is interpreting the incident. "You like to be late?"

"This isn't about that. Come on, you weren't even late. It must be tough on her, living with a guy who won't let the small stuff go."

A glimmer of understanding lights Mark's face. As much as he wants to reject it, the point of Tom's message is slowly seeping through. "Funny, I'm always telling her to let the small stuff go."

With a gentle smile, Tom nods. "That's a tough way to go. You've got to let go of that garbage. You've got to forgive her for that kind of junk. Neither of you is perfect. You want forgiveness, right? Don't you appreciate grace when you've messed something up? I do! Don't expect it if you don't give it."

Mark shrugs and adds in a sincere tone, "Tom, I do forgive her. At least I think I do. I try."

Tom points to his temple. "You've got to take it from here," he moves his finger down and taps his heart, "to here."

Mark's gaze shifts to the ground. There is a momentary pause as he digests the information.

"If you don't," Tom adds, "it'll swallow up your marriage and destroy you both."

Up to this point we have spent a lot of time defining the elements that establish marital bliss. As we proceed on our journey we will examine the damage that results when a marriage is not running on all cylinders. We will also look at some ways to start the healing process within yourself and your marriage. Let's begin by looking at a concept that has so many false beliefs attached to it that some people find it impossible to carry out. We are talking about forgiveness.

For some of you, even the idea of forgiveness leaves a bad taste in your mouth. Let's dispel some of the common misconceptions and redefine it based on what Scripture says and why it is essential. Understand that this is a topic entire books could be (and have been) dedicated to. We will establish a working understanding of forgiveness and how it should be applied in your marriage and other relationships as well.

THE COMMAND TO FORGIVE

In the Lord's Prayer, a model for praying given to the disciples by Jesus, we read,

> Forgive us our debts, as we also have forgiven our debtors…
>
> Matthew 6:12

This is a command to forgive those who have wronged us as we have been forgiven by God for our own transgressions. As we go further in that same chapter, we read,

> For if you forgive men when they sin against you,
> your heavenly Father will also forgive you. But if
> you do not forgive men their sins, your father will
> not forgive your sins.
>
>   Matthew 6:14-15

Why does Jesus make such a definitive statement? The primary reason lies in the fact that for us to deny forgiveness to another is arrogance on our part. It's as if we are denying that we too are sinners and in need of God's forgiveness every bit as much as that other person. How much more when you withhold forgiveness from your spouse. God views forgiveness as a necessary element within our relationships.

You have probably asked yourself, "How many times am I supposed to forgive that knothead? It seems like they just keep repeating the same things that cause me so much pain." Granted, that statement may well define exactly how you feel right now. Your emotions may be stretched tight, and you might not care for the answer. I present it to you with no regrets since the answer is not really mine. Look up Matthew 18:21-22. What does it tell you about forgiveness? The message is pretty clear. Peter had a set number of times in his head before he would be justified in cutting off someone he considered his enemy. Jesus tells Peter that, unlike what the spiritual leaders of the day taught, our forgiveness should be infinite. This is not to say there aren't times when we should set boundaries to eliminate repeated intentional hurts by another.

You see, in those days the people were taught by the spiritual leaders that those who offend should be forgiven only three times. Jesus tells Peter to have a heart of perpetual forgiveness. Part of the problem people have with forgiveness lies in the messages we are often taught growing up such as, "You need to forgive and forget," or "Forgiveness is complete when things are made right."

WHY FORGIVENESS?

First of all let's look at why God says to forgive. We can all agree about the power anger can have over an individual. If left unchecked it resides in us like a cancer, and some in the medical professions believe it could even be a cause of cancer, but many other issues are related to unresolved anger.

We spend much of our time despising what someone has done to us. We spend much of the day looking for other things to add fuel to that fire in order to justify the pain caused by that anger. Anger takes a firm root and grows. It seeps into other areas of our lives as well, affecting our general disposition. We can become a bear to be around. You see, the problem is that anger envelops our heart and we become a bitter person. It is imperative to forgive because if not we become stuck and unable to move forward in our lives. Essentially we give control to the offending person for our behavior. Do you really want to give that much control to someone who has already hurt you so deeply? Certainly not!

Forgiveness is a way for you to acknowledge what has happened, relinquish the power of the anger and hurt, and move forward.

Some of us believe it is necessary to forget the damage done to us once we have forgiven. We think that otherwise true forgiveness is not possible. Think of forgiveness as a journey that begins with the decision to take the trip. We must decide to move along the path of holiness toward emotional healing from the pain inflicted. Once we decide to forgive it does not mean the emotional damage will simply disappear. At times you may remember the incident that caused the pain, but that does not mean you haven't forgiven. The remembrance just means the pain has not yet gone away. It may be necessary to give it back to God so that you do not dwell on that pain. It may take some time for your emotional healing to catch up to your spiritual decision, depending on the degree of the damage, but remind yourself that you have decided to forgive and that God will give you the strength to move forward.

Forgiveness does not mean you will simply forget what has happened in the past. What it does mean is that you can decide how much control it will have on your future. Merriam-Webster defines the word *forget* as "to disregard intentionally." Again we come back to intentionality. We must choose to leave the *pain* of the past at the foot of the cross or we will continue to be re-victimized over and over as we allow the bitterness back in.

We must also understand that our ability to forgive may have nothing to do with whether the situation is resolved or all wrongs are righted. If God tells us we should forgive, that means it is something we have the ability to do regardless of the actions of others. In some cases the other person may not believe (or choose not to accept responsibility) that they even committed the offense that hurt you so deeply. This is common in cases of molestation.

This brings up a good point. I have worked with people who were molested in their younger years and now as adults request help and healing so they can get on with their lives. In some instances the perpetrator is deceased. Forgiveness is a key element in our ability to move beyond our pain. But how on earth can we possibly forgive the perpetrator if we have no ability to get restitution? By understanding that God does not make restitution a condition of our ability to forgive. The choice to begin the forgiveness journey resides in the decision you make between God and yourself.

Ephesians 5:1 tells us to "be imitators of God, therefore, as dearly loved children and live a life of love, just as Christ loved us and gave himself up for us...." We are called to be imitators of God. We are called to extend ourselves beyond our own understanding, beyond our own emotional hurts, and behave in ways that will edify one another and grow our marriages.

Sometimes moving beyond the pain of the past is not directly related to your relationship with your spouse. The pain can come from much further back in your life experiences. The problem with unresolved forgiveness is that it creates a root of dysfunction that infiltrates the garden of your marital relationship. Now we will hear from a woman I had the honor of counseling many years ago who endured horrendous abuse while growing up. This testimony will demonstrate that, albeit more difficult in certain situations, forgiveness is nonetheless the necessary salve to heal wounds that can prevent you from having healthy relationships.

In Their Own Words: Extending the Grace of Forgiveness

My husband and I have now been married for nine years. A good marriage doesn't come easy, especially when I was carrying a lot of baggage from my childhood. During our first year of marriage, I was still angry, bitter, and resentful. I misdirected those feelings onto my husband. I was impatient, sarcastic, and overly sensitive, acting like a selfish brat. I yelled, trying to control certain situations, since in my childhood I had had no control. These were definitely bad behaviors.

My father was an alcoholic and womanizer who used to curse and beat our mother. Every Sunday the car trips to Grandma's would end up in fighting, with Dad driving drunk back home. I remember crying quietly in fear that we would die in a car crash. I never received a hug or word of love or approval from him, only anger and beatings with a belt. I was very insecure and fearful.

Then things got a lot worse. For at the age of ten, my father began molesting me sexually. He fed me a lot of guilt and said that I would hurt my mother if I told her. The shame, guilt, brainwashing, and fear kept me locked in that ugly dark secret.

Needing and seeking approval and love, I became pregnant at the age of seventeen. He too was abusive, alcoholic, and unfaithful. After twenty years of marriage, and when my children were old enough, I divorced him. It was only then at the age of forty-one, after my mother passed away, that I told any living soul (a counselor) about my hidden secret of sexual abuse. I thought my life would miraculously change. Obviously it did not.

I continued my emotionally unhealthy life, dating abusive, alcoholic men. I then began drinking to be accepted and more fun. Maybe that would help them to love me, I thought. One day I knew I needed help and went to a Codependents Anonymous meeting and was led to a Women of Abuse group. I learned I didn't have to accept abuse of any kind. Learning to love myself was difficult.

Years later, meeting my husband was in God's plan and in his timing. It didn't come easy accepting the love he had for me. Our premarital counseling took a bit longer than usual. After a time, my premarital counselor referred me to another Christian counselor, a woman who specialized in working with the wounded child in me. Months of counseling helped me work through many issues. I am still learning and healing; however, I don't live in fear of abuse or abandonment anymore. Because of God's perfect love, I have learned to love myself and accept love from others.

In the beginning of our marriage, it was very hard for me to be a godly wife. "Submit to my husband? Oh, no way!" I was not going to be controlled, not even a little. My spouse came from a Christian home. His parents just celebrated fifty-one years of marriage, so I had resentment toward him for having a better life than I did. I would yell at him, "You'll never be able to understand all that I went through." *We* never fought, but *I* did. I would pick fights, but he would never engage in them. My behavior was that of a stubborn, selfish, demanding child. My husband, being rooted in God's Word, would quote Scripture to me when I was angry and out of control, trying to help calm me down. That only angered me all the more, thus making our lives miserable. Like a spoiled child not getting my way, I would shut down and isolate.

Because of my insecurities, almost every time we were on our way to a church function or get-togethers with friends and family, I would create drama with the hope that we would cancel. His endurance and patience would win out and we would go and ultimately have a good time. I now realized why I behaved that way. He was my husband, mine, and I did not want to share him.

I came to realize that I had to do something about a massive destructive root in my life. It became necessary to do something I never thought I could do: I needed to forgive my father, with no expectations from him. This was extremely hard to do, but I knew God was calling me (and all of us) to forgive in order to be free of the anger, bitterness, and hate that had kept me living in my pain all those years. When I gave him forgiveness, I was freed. I was no longer hiding in the darkest days of my life. It was all in the light now. I have since been able to enjoy a life of freedom, to love others, to be myself as God intended me to be, to laugh and live a good life blessed by Him. Life isn't perfect, but these days I would say pretty close. Yes, I was robbed, cheated, and hurt, but if I hadn't forgiven my father I would have robbed myself of the last twelve years, the best years of my life.

My husband gave me grace and still continues to, even when I'm not sure I deserved it, because he too receives grace from God. I have never known such joy as I have in my life now. As for that inner-child I was talking about, that girl who needed so much healing. She is now a Sunday school teacher and she gets to play with the five-year-olds at our church. What fun! Thank you, Jesus.

TAKING ACTION

Exercise 5.1   What If... Forgiveness

In your marriage are you following what 1 Corinthians 13:5 says with regard to love, "...it keeps no record of wrongs"? If you followed the practice of forgiveness, how might your marriage change? Think about the possibilities if you were able to let go of those past hurts.

Now you will have the opportunity to practice the fine art of forgiveness. This is something that both you and your spouse will do individually. Remember that extending forgiveness to your mate is a process you share with God.

Exercise 5.2   My Forgiveness Letter (Extending Forgiveness to My Spouse)

Find yourself a nice secluded place. It doesn't matter where you go as long as you can have a place to concentrate. Have plenty of paper on hand. Do not write this exercise in this book or your journal. It may take more than one sitting to complete this assignment, and you don't want anyone to read this letter. Begin this process by praying that God would give you the strength and courage to address the pain and hurt that will likely surface as you start to write your list of hurts.

Address the letter to your spouse and then follow it with your statement of forgiveness: "I choose to forgive you for…" No doubt several feelings will surface. Identify the pain that would interfere with your ability to forgive. Write down the first emotional responses to your statement of forgiveness. In other words, how do you feel about the idea of forgiving your spouse for this issue. Write down the second emotional response, then the third. Write them all out, beginning each time with "I choose to forgive you for…" Let them flow.

Continue writing until all that you feel is written on the paper before you. This process will help to move some of these destructive, hurtful feelings out of you and into the open, much as a surgeon tries to cut away anything that would interfere with the normal functioning of your body. Feel free to write as much as you need to write. Once you have addressed all the feelings that surfaced from your first statement of forgiveness, take a breath and write "I forgive you" for a final time regarding that issue.

Example:

Dear Jim,

I forgive you for not making me a priority in our relationship.
- *Why am I bothering to forgive you? You couldn't care less!*
- *I'll never have priority over your friends.*
- *I hate it when you work all the time and have no time for me!*
- *It embarrasses and hurts me when I hear how my friends' husbands enjoy time with their wives.*

I forgive you for not making me a priority in our relationship.

Now we move on to your next statement of forgiveness. Write "I forgive you for..." and go through the same process as just described. You will continue to move through all the issues you have been harboring resentment about, letting them go one by one by extending forgiveness for them.

When you feel that you have addressed everything you want to cover in your letter, take a moment to reflect on what you have just completed. Do not feel that you must complete this in one sitting, as the emotions generated by this assignment may require that you revisit it a couple of times to complete it.

Exercise 5.3   Sharing My Forgiveness Letter

We follow this letter with a technique that allows you to receive closure in those areas that you need to forgive in your spouse. It is known as "the empty chair technique." Take a seat next to another chair and imagine that your spouse is sitting there, willing to receive what you wrote in your letter. Read the letter aloud to them, and each time you make your statement of forgiveness, imagine your spouse accepting your forgiveness. Take as long as necessary to complete this process.

Once you have shared your letter of forgiveness, destroy it thoroughly. There is no need to actually share it with your spouse or to keep it on hand to revisit. It is done; now let it go. This is an issue between God and yourself. If the enemy tries to throw it back up in your face, remind yourself that you are done harboring resentment about that and have given it to God.

Now that you have concluded this assignment, do not take back what you have extended. It's time to leave the hurt at the foot of the cross and go forward on your journey of forgiveness. Is there anyone else in your life that has hurt you? Is there anyone else you need to forgive? It would benefit you to go through this process again, addressing those other people toward whom you have developed bitterness. God wants your yoke to be light. It's time to let go of the anger so that you focus your energy toward what God has planned for you instead. Please do not proceed further in this book until you have completed this assignment.

Notes to Self—
Forgiveness, Ugh!

Part II:

Building the Relationship

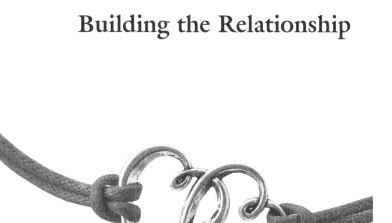

Chapter Six

Building a Foundation of Intimacy

Whenever someone experiences car trouble, one of two things must occur. First, if you have been blessed with a mechanical aptitude, you will pop the hood and do a step-by-step analysis to determine the problem, then repair accordingly. Second, if you fall into the category of people of which I am a member, you will call your mechanic to have them take a look at the situation. The experts will evaluate and diagnose the problem and make any repairs necessary to your car, hopefully putting it back into the state prior to the breakdown. Marriage is very much the same way. When things start to break down it becomes necessary to evaluate and repair the relationship. The great thing is that if both spouses are willing to put forth the effort, complete reparation is possible. We need to remind ourselves of what kind of God we serve. He is the God of miracles. He is also a healing God, and a God of restoration.

In the book of Amos, Israel is being punished for falling into sin, and the house of David has fallen. God had made a covenant with David, stating that one of his descendants would always sit on the throne. In Amos 9:11, God declares, "I will restore David's fallen tent, I will repair its broken places, restore its ruins, and will rebuild it as it used to be...." You and your spouse have also made a covenant with that same God. If you will allow him to lead, he will take your marriage on a journey of restoration like you never thought possible. But remember, it will be necessary for you to slide over and let God take the wheel.

Okay, so we (or our reliable mechanic) have the hood open and have been tinkering around; we have identified a few (or perhaps many) problematic issues with your vehicle. Now the goal is to put things right. Let's begin the same process for our marriage, shall we? Let's take a look at some foundational elements that are common to a healthy, thriving marriage. The following are ways to increase intimacy by implementing some shared activities.

In the following pages, identify where you view your relationship in the twelve categories, and think about ways you can improve what you are doing now. Remember, if your relationship is experiencing some difficulties, the first reaction is to want to cite all the areas in which your spouse is failing. That is not what we are going to do. You are responsible for your behavior and your spouse is responsible for theirs, so let them address themselves in their book and you address your behavior here. When you have finished, sit down together and share how you assessed the relationship in these areas and the ways you would like to improve in those areas. If you need extra space feel free to complete this exercise on a few separate sheets of paper, or use your own journal.

CREATING INTIMACY

As with anything else, identifying areas that need to improve and actually putting forth the efforts to improve are two different things. Now you need to make the decision to change and act on it! Ask God to give you the strength, courage, and healing to put these new improvements into practice.

Worship has to be on the top of the list. It is a broad category that includes attending church together, praying together, and reading the Bible together. There are other ways of worshipping together, but we will narrow our focus to these facets. *Church attendance* is very important as an outward expression of what you believe. The teachings serve to offer new input into your mind and soul. New input can challenge those unhealthy thoughts and at least give opportunity for change. Second Corinthians 10:5 states, "We demolish arguments and every pretension that sets itself up against the knowledge of God, and we take captive every thought to make it obedient to Christ."

How would this be possible if we don't know the knowledge of God? This is my personal life verse, and I highly recommend that you commit it to memory as a reminder. Get yourself plugged into a congregation that will challenge you. If you are sick, you go to the doctor, because he is the expert and authority. God is the expert and authority on marriage, and since he designed it, it would behoove you to find out what he has to say.

Praying together is a surefire way to increase intimacy in your relationship. You sit before God together, searching his heart and what he wants for the two of you. You don't have to feel obligated to fill the air with words. You can keep your prayers simple and heartfelt. Sit together and listen—listen to what God would stir in your heart. Ask God to show you the things you need to change. But be careful; if you ask God to show you yourself, he will, so be ready to receive what he has to say. Remember he only wants you to be the best you can be, the way he created you.

The best and simplest way to visualize how God fits into the marriage commitment is as follows: envision a pyramid. At the top of the pyramid is God, the designer of marriage. He is at the pinnacle of the triangle. At the bottom left angle of the triangle we find the husband. At the bottom right angle we find his lovely wife. Now, place one finger on each bottom angle, representing the husband and the wife. Slowly slide your fingers up the sides of the triangle, moving toward the name God. What do you notice? As you move closer to God, you move closer to each other. Point taken?

Reading the Word together has great marital benefits as well. It sparks great conversations as you contemplate what God would speak to you through the Scriptures. It provides a time for growing together in Him, which in turn increases intimacy. You will also get to know your spouse better as you share thoughts on God's insights.

Fellowship with like believers is a key component to a successful relationship as well. One of the many benefits is accountability. It is important to have other people in your lives who will help keep you on track. You need people in your lives who have permission to speak truth to you, people you trust and who want what is best for you and your marriage. Both couples should share the same beliefs and moral foundations. Without a similar moral base, the counsel offered will likely be in conflict or at best inconsistent to what is in the best interest of the marriage.

> A friend loves at all times, and a brother is born for adversity.
>
> Proverbs 17:17

Each of you needs to have friends of the same sex that you can bounce things off of before you open your mouth about some irrational feelings that are more likely to harm rather than help your spouse. The phrase "friends of the same sex" was used with deliberate consideration. The last thing a troubled relationship needs is one spouse seeking consolation in the arms of the opposite sex. This is common with men who don't understand there is nothing more confirming (and attractive) to a woman than a man who is willing to be open and honest about their feelings and share them.

Unfortunately, if the woman is having troubles in her own marriage she will most likely view the attention as an open invitation. The man may "innocently" view it as a way to release some of his frustration and be consoled by a woman who cares about him. The wife who shares with a male friend, co-worker, or boss may be thrilled at the idea of having a man who actually hears her and affirms her feelings.

One of the elements of a healthy marital relationship that is all too often eliminated once the ring goes on the finger is *date night*. It is amazing how many couples don't remember the last time they and their spouse did something together by themselves. Realizing that once the adorable little kiddies come things can be a bit difficult and schedules fill up fast does not make it less important.

Perhaps it would be good to view your relationship the same way you view your career or work life. How do we get things done at work? We prioritize the workload. This may seem very mechanical and even uncaring, but doesn't the lack of prioritizing your marital life strike you as being considerably less caring? For the guys, take the initiative and set up a babysitter, make a dinner reservation, make all the arrangements. Trust me, she will appreciate it. A word of advice: don't make the movies your destination unless it's the rare exception. That in itself does not classify as a date night. Conversation and interaction is limited between a couple while the THX sound is blaring in their eardrums.

Ladies, you too have a great ability to orchestrate wonderful getaways and weekend excursions; use that gifting. Not everything you do need be expensive. For those on a budget, a walk in the park, a long drive, or a field by the airport to watch the planes take off would all do nicely. Both of you, be creative! My wife and I have Disneyland passes and love to go there on a Sunday night, ride a few rides, and have a nice dinner, but mostly it affords us opportunity to chat as we stroll around the park. If you don't give your marriage priority, I promise you the odds of finding yourself available are great.

Supporting your spouse is another element in creating a satisfying marriage. Whether it's a matter of simply validating your spouse by listening to what they have to say or financially backing your wife's new book—and everything in between—your spouse needs to know that you are an active partner. You do not have to agree with everything your spouse says, but the very least you can do is hear them out and weigh the pros and cons of their proposal. Many things will require seeking the Lord for direction, so take that time and be encouraging to your partner. Remember, it's not all about you; your spouse has a thought process that is just as valid as yours.

In the same vein, it's important to **acknowledge the efforts of your spouse**. All too often we take our wives or husbands for granted. Does that sound familiar? Perhaps you heard it from your spouse this week. Don't do that! The world offers plenty of opportunity to tear down your mate. Acknowledging good behavior is one of the most effective ways to elicit change in a person. Think about it. With children, how do you get them to do the things you want them to do? Whether it's doing their chores, being polite, or sharing their toys, we encourage them when they do what is right. "Thank you Johnny; Mommy really appreciates it when you take out the trash." "Susie, that was very nice of you to let your sister play with your doll."

Positive reinforcement makes such a big difference. And it's not just the children; we all appreciate it when our efforts are recognized. The best way to encourage long-term change in our loved ones is to acknowledge them and make them aware that we appreciate what they are doing. Leave it alone and don't say anything and you have ensured that the positive behaviors will stop in short order.

Going through trials together certainly builds intimacy in a relationship. The interesting thing about trials is that they often force greater reliance on God, thereby offering an opportunity to grow in our faith.

> We do not want to be uninformed, brothers, about the hardships we suffered in the province of Asia. We were under great pressure, far beyond our ability to endure, so that we despaired even of life. Indeed, in our hearts we felt the sentence of death. But this happened that we might not rely on ourselves but on God, who raises the dead.
>
> 2 Corinthians 1:8-9

Sometimes the trials that couples go through are incredibly difficult. When two people are on the same page and working toward the same ends, the pain is considerably reduced by having someone to share them with. It is essential that couples be willing to share difficult circumstances with one another. Men are notorious for stuffing situations so as not to trouble their wives. Let your wife see inside you and understand your troubles; let her encourage and support you. If something is bothering you, odds are that you will make it known whether you say anything or not. When you become quiet or grumpy, your spouse will suspect that something is wrong. This leaves the spouse to feel responsible for your behavior when it may have nothing at all to do with them. If there are only two people in a room and one of them is obviously upset, it stands to reason that the remaining person must have done something to offend the other. This is often how people think, whether it's accurate or not.

When couples have the opportunity to work problems through to resolution together, they feel a great sense of accomplishment and it strengthens the marriage. Remember, you guys are a team. Play like one!

When couples *work together to reach mutual goals*, the level of intimacy increases in the marriage. A great deal of satisfaction comes from accomplishments made as a team. Look at the excitement and energy on display when a baseball team wins an important game. They train, struggle, and sweat together to take that championship. Listen to the guys sharing about their last backpacking trip and the satisfaction expressed that in spite of fatigue, terrain, or weather conditions, they made it to their destination together. Observe the young couple who scrimped and saved prior to getting married just so they would have enough money to make a down payment on their first home. The joy of accomplishment is beyond words!

Working together toward a common goal creates a sense of belonging, teamwork, and accomplishment, there is no doubt. It is important to benchmark goals and have smaller intermediary goals on the way to the grand finale of goals. By doing so, momentum will remain high because we can see our efforts beginning to pay off, thus increasing the likelihood of attaining our end goal.

SETTING GOALS TOGETHER

An acronym that helps to summarize the basics of goal setting is as follows. Goals should be S.M.A.R.T.

Goals should be Specific. The problem with the goals many people set is that they are so vague it is difficult to determine the direction the goal setting is headed. Leave for your destination without a map and only a vague idea of where you're headed and you will end up traveling all over town and wasting a great deal of gasoline and time in the process—to say nothing of the frustration and anger that will result. A map shows us exactly where we are headed, and we'll know when we arrive.

Goals should be Measurable. It is helpful to have a way to benchmark our productivity as we move toward a goal. In this way we can assess from time to time and see if we are indeed moving along the right road. When a goal is measurable we are also encouraged by the small plateaus we hit in striving toward the desired end.

Goals should be Achievable. We should not set financial goals so high that we will never meet the mark. A family with a combined annual income of $50,000 should probably not decide to start saving $2000 a month toward a down payment for a new home. They will become disheartened by the second month and give up the goal entirely.

Goals should be Realistic. It's great to be a visionary, but if you set your goals too lofty you will never be able to attain them. You will simply become frustrated and give up.

Goals should be Time Sensitive. We should make sure that we designate a certain amount of time for accomplishing our goals. This too will help us to benchmark our progress. Short-term goals are usually ones that you can successfully accomplish in six months to one year's time. Longer-term goals will usually range from one to five years.

Again, your goals can be personal ones, something you would like to accomplish. Maybe the completion of that college degree you have been working on, or joining the gym to take off those last ten pounds. They can be goals focused on you and your mate—perhaps saving some money so that you can attend an upcoming marriage retreat your church is sponsoring. Goals can also be family oriented, such as putting together a big family vacation. When we are working toward the same goals as a couple or family, we get to share in the benefits of accomplishment.

Finding things to do together as a couple shows your spouse that you are interested and find value in the time spent together. If you do not currently participate in activities together, begin to find like interests you can share. In some cases that may be a tall task. Perhaps you have difficulty finding things that interest you both. I had absolutely no desire to see the Meryl Streep film *The Devil Wears Prada* when it debuted. Mind you, I love movies, but this was not my idea of an evening's entertainment. I chose not to operate in my feelings but to step out of the box and do something for my wife. When she asked, I bit the bullet. "Why sure, honey. I'd love to go see it." We went out for dinner then off to the movie. I simply changed my mindset. I wasn't going to see *The Devil Wears Prada*, I was taking the opportunity to spend some time with my wife. It all worked out just fine, and the movie wasn't bad either.

Practicing selfless love is a great way to grow your relationship. Although the activities may be fun, it's more important that you begin to view them as time you get to spend with your spouse. This will make the activities that are not so interesting to you personally just as enjoyable. You can alternate activities, taking turns picking what you will do. Husband, you agree to take in the new chick flick or some such activity, then next week the wife agrees to go to the NASCAR races. Remember, the activity is not as important as the time spent together.

Fulfilling your sexual commitments in marriage is another foundation to establishing intimacy. Depending on how severe the difficulties in your marriage, you will either welcome or cringe at that statement. Listen, whether you wish to repair your marriage or simply do a little marriage enhancement, the issue is stepping out of yourself and doing the right thing. Again, a rewarding marriage requires effort on both spouses.

> The husband should fulfill his marital duty to his wife, and likewise the wife to her husband.
>
> 1 Corinthians 7:3

If the husband and wife are not fulfilling one another sexually it opens the door to satisfaction outside of the marital bed. Lack of sexual fulfillment can open the opportunity for pornography, sexting, extramarital affairs, and any number of ways that the world pushes against marriages by offering alternatives to your spouse. Let's look further in the Scripture:

> The wife's body does not belong to her alone but also to her husband. In the same way, the husband's body does not belong to him alone but also to his wife.
>
> 1 Corinthians 7:4

So we see that in the marital commitment we give ourselves to the other, the idea of two becoming as one. As a couple we have an obligation to care for one another. Withholding sex from your spouse as a means of punishment does nothing but cause further destruction to the marriage.

Creating your own family traditions is a great way to draw the entire family closer together. You may enjoy the planning and preparation of yearly vacations together. Let the entire family come up with activities they would like to do at vacation time; that way everybody participates and feels like they have input into the family. There are many ways you can go with this category—be creative!

More than a year before we got married, my wife often repeated her dream of starting a new ritual when we had children. She envisioned the Disney Family Christmas Hat Parade. We would all gather on Christmas morning, sit at the dining room table, and make hats out of construction paper and whatever goodies we had around the house. On completion, we would take out toy instruments, wear our fancy new hats, and parade around the house. One of the joys of having a sanguine wife is that sometimes these ideas pass swiftly. Naturally, my fear is that once she reads this book, it will reignite that flame. Pray for me.

I love going out to breakfast with one of my sons once a week. Granted, he's five but he loves the time spent together and he has plenty to talk about. These are just a couple of examples. Come up with things that will be unique to your family. Let the entire family participate. This is a great way for members of the family to feel like they are heard and valued.

Sharing household responsibilities is a great way to demonstrate teamwork. Here again you can be creative. You don't need to live by traditional roles. In this day and age you see fewer traditional roles within families since many women work outside the home to help make ends meet. Whereas the home was once the woman's domain and the workplace the man's domain, not so much the case these days. Both parties reside in the home, so there is no reason that both parties can't help keep the home front together.

Things operate best if everyone is allowed to flow within their giftings. If the wife has an aptitude for money matters, let her be the one responsible for the household bills. The husband may love doing the dishes. Fine, make that his responsibility. Maybe you both love giving the kids their baths and getting them ready for bed. Go for it! By sharing these responsibilities all the burden is not placed on just one of the spouses. You both get to share the benefit of a clean and organized home.

Allowing for individual time to pursue the interests that you and your spouse enjoy separately cultivates trust and selflessness in a relationship. The time spent doing the things you enjoy as an individual is just as important as the time you spend as a couple. For one thing, it is a great opportunity to develop friendships, which is a key element in accountability. For another, it gives a certain freedom to your spouse when you allow them time to engage in what they enjoy. They come back to the relationship with a longing to engage with you. You will never know how much you love and appreciate your spouse if you never give them time away from you.

There is a necessary balance between the time spent together and time apart. Be encouraging when you give your mate the time away, and don't do it grudgingly. If you want them to come back refreshed and happy to see you, don't send them off with a guilt trip.

Creating times to celebrate is one way that a couple (and family) can draw closer together. Obvious examples are birthdays, anniversaries, and graduations—all times when one spouse can go out of their way to recognize and edify the other. Husbands, your beautiful wife may tell you, "Don't get me anything for my birthday this year," or "Christmas should be for the children; let's just spend whatever we were going to spend on each other and buy something special for the kids." Take my advice: even if they say not to, show them how much you love them by giving them a token of that love. That gesture will show them that you consider them to be a priority in your life.

Celebrate the payoff of your home mortgage, reaching a mutual weight loss goal, a promotion at work, and anything that shows how working as a team pays off. Make that extra effort to show your spouse how special they are to you.

TAKING ACTION

Exercise 6.1   Assessing the Thirteen Areas of Intimacy

Consider the areas of intimacy described in this chapter. How do you measure up? Where can you improve? Complete this exercise as an individual project.

1) Worshipping together:
How do we measure up as a couple?

Poor   1 2 3 4 5 6 7 8 9 10   **Great**

Where could we improve?

What will my effort be in making improvements in this area?

2) Fellowshipping with other believers:
How do we measure up as a couple?

Poor   1 2 3 4 5 6 7 8 9 10   **Great**

Where could we improve?

What will my effort be in making improvements in this area?

3) Having date nights:
How do we measure up as a couple?

Poor   1 2 3 4 5 6 7 8 9 10   **Great**

Where could we improve?

What will my effort be in making improvements in this area?

4) Supporting your spouse:
How do we measure up as a couple?

Poor   1 2 3 4 5 6 7 8 9 10   **Great**

Where could we improve?

What will my effort be in making improvements in this area?

5) Acknowledging the efforts of your spouse:
How do we measure up as a couple?

Poor   1 2 3 4 5 6 7 8 9 10   **Great**

Where could we improve?

What will my effort be in making improvements in this area?

6) Going through trials together:
How do we measure up as a couple?

Poor   1 2 3 4 5 6 7 8 9 10   **Great**

Where could we improve?

What will my effort be in making improvements in this area?

7) Working together to reach mutual goals:
How do we measure up as a couple?

Poor   1 2 3 4 5 6 7 8 9 10   **Great**

Where could we improve?
What will my effort be in making improvements in this area?

8) Finding things to do as a couple:
How do we measure up as a couple?
    Poor   1 2 3 4 5 6 7 8 9 10   **Great**
Where could we improve?
What will my effort be in making improvements in this area?

9) Fulfilling your sexual commitments:
How do we measure up as a couple?
    Poor   1 2 3 4 5 6 7 8 9 10   **Great**
Where could we improve?
What will my effort be in making improvements in this area?

10) Creating your own family traditions:
How do we measure up as a couple?
    Poor   1 2 3 4 5 6 7 8 9 10   **Great**
Where could we improve?
What will my effort be in making improvements in this area?

11) Sharing household responsibilities:
How do we measure up as a couple?
    Poor   1 2 3 4 5 6 7 8 9 10   **Great**
Where could we improve?
What will my effort be in making improvements in this area?

12) Allowing for individual time:
How do we measure up as a couple?
    Poor   1 2 3 4 5 6 7 8 9 10   **Great**
Where could we improve?
What will my effort be in making improvements in this area?

13) Creating times to celebrate:
How do we measure up as a couple?
   Poor   1 2 3 4 5 6 7 8 9 10   **Great**
Where could we improve?
What will my effort be in making improvements in this area?

Set aside a time to share with one another how you sized up the marriage based on these intimacy issues. Compare notes and see if there is some common ground, then agree to work on it together. Write up a plan on how you will each work as a couple toward changing the dynamics of the intimacy in your relationship.

Exercise 6.2   Let's Set Some Goals
Take some time and individually make a list of five goals for you and your spouse.

Now take your list and share it with your spouse. Pick one or two of the items that you see on both lists that have similarities and create a common goal that you can both work toward as a team. Assess every so often to see if you are headed in the right direction, and reward yourselves for your efforts.

Exercise 6.3   What Activities Do I Enjoy?
For this exercise prepare a list of twenty-five activities you really enjoy (or think you might) and would love doing with your spouse. Again, these activities may be ones that you have never attempted but would love to do with your mate, or simply things you already enjoy doing. Remember, the goal is to use this list when we are finding things to do together as a couple.

Once you have both completed your list of activities, make a photocopy of it. Exchange lists with each other. Your mate will love it when you plan a day doing something they really enjoy, and this will show them how much you care for them. This will also eliminate the statement "I don't know…what do you want to do?" when you begin to plan date nights.

Notes to Self—
Building a Foundation of Intimacy

_____

_____

_____

_____

_____

_____

_____

_____

_____

_____

_____

_____

_____

_____

_____

_____

_____

_____

_____

_____

_____

_____

_____

Chapter Seven

The Differences Between Us

Mark enters through the front door and sets his briefcase in the foyer. After flinging off his jacket and hanging it on the coat hook, he rushes into the living room. Sheila is coming down the hall from Alex's room. She turns off the hall light switch. Mark grunts in disappointment.

Sheila smiles. "It's okay. I just put him down."

Mark grins as he proceeds to Alex's room, but not before grabbing Sheila by the shoulders and giving her a peck on the lips. "After I give the big boy a kiss goodnight I want to talk."

Sheila looks pleased that Mark is initiating the conversation. Perhaps the new marriage counseling is taking hold. She's noticed some definite changes in Mark's attitude as of late.

Moments later he comes into the living room, smiling from ear to ear.

"What's going on?" Sheila queries.

Mark reaches for his jacket pocket, forgetting that he hung it up in a hurry to kiss Alex goodnight. "Oh." He points his finger to the curious Sheila. "Be right back!" He rushes to the foyer, throws open his jacket, and pulls out an envelope of some sort. Placing the surprise envelope behind him, he rushes back to his suspecting wife. She takes a sip of coffee. "Okay, what is this?"

Mark hands the envelope to her. "Surprise!"

She opens the envelope and removes airline tickets. She reads them and a serious expression comes over her face. "What are these for? We're not going to Chicago. We can't."

"Why can't we? You've been talking about wanting to see your family. Alex has never been to Chicago."

Confused, Sheila is at a loss. "We can't just fly off to Chicago for a week. This is something that has to be planned!"

Mark is a bit surprised by Sheila's response. "It's perfect! Alex is on vacation. You don't have any assignments over the next two weeks. I can take Alex to see the Bears play."

Sheila displays her displeasure. "We can't just pick up and take off on a whim."

"You are the one who said I'm never spontaneous and I've gotten very selfish in our marriage. Do you remember saying that to the counselor? I'm trying to do something just for you. Let me do it." Mark smiles like a little puppy.

Sheila snaps at him as if he were a child, "You don't just do something like this. You don't know how to plan this."

Mark's smile begins to fade. "Believe it or not, I did. I'm not an idiot."

"We have to make sure that Alex has the right clothes. It's cold in Chicago."

Mark feels beat down. "So we go clothes shopping and get a few things."

"Where are we going to stay?

"I talked to your Aunt June and she is very excited." He puts his head down as he turns from her. "I thought you would be too. Everything doesn't have to be on an agenda. Maybe you need to learn to go with the flow."

Feeling remorse for her abrupt actions, Sheila tries to make things right. "I'm sorry, Mark. I guess I'm just not used to you taking the initiative, and this is such a big thing. I don't think you are an idiot. I just have to work on letting go of the control. Can we start this conversation again?"

Mark turns back toward Sheila, and his smile is a better response than any words.

As we age and mature, the hope is that we grow emotionally and spiritually. Unfortunately for many, myself included, we also grow physically. No matter how much we try to push, tuck, cram, and squeeze we will never get into the jeans of our youth. Face it, size 32 jeans were not designed to accommodate 40-inch waists, no matter what you want to believe! Some people try to do the same thing with their spouses.

How God Created Men and Women

It is a great mistake to try to force our wives or husbands into a mold of our own design. Develop the understanding that your differences are ideally the things that strengthen a marriage. What is required to make it work is a measure of patience, grace, and humility. On this leg of our journey we will identify what makes a man and a woman tick. As we go deeper, we will uncover the heart of both men and women. Let's begin by taking a look at some typical characteristics. These characteristics may not run completely across the board with every man or woman, but they are typical enough that we need to acknowledge these traits to better understand the person we married.

For men, the desire *to be appreciated* is a key factor. We like to know that our presence in a situation has an impact on that situation. We want to know that our input makes a difference. Men also tend to be *competitive* by nature. The challenge (and the fun) of winning is in the race. Even though maturing means we have to accept the occasional loss, no man likes it.

A couple made the decision to take off a few pounds. They signed up for Weight Watchers and began their point system for weight loss. It's a well-known fact that men lose weight at a faster rate than women do—one of the things the husband greatly anticipated. Sure enough, the first week he lost 7.4 pounds and his wife lost considerably less than that, no big surprise. It was not because he was doing so much better than she but because of how men and women's body chemistry and metabolism works. Frankly, he didn't care about the reason as long as he continued to beat her. This simple example makes a point. Men love the thrill of the competition; it's how we're wired. As a rule men care less about the details and more about the finish line.

Women love the *joy of anticipation*, so they typically like the idea of planning ahead. For some, the thought process, the discussions, and the planning are the most rewarding part of the execution of events. Women tend to have a more *cooperative nature*, so they enjoy the opportunity to work with others. You can see why that would be important to a woman in her relationship. This is why the husband that "shuts down" is a painful hurdle for the wife to get over.

Men have a *"fix-it" mentality*. They like the challenge of addressing a problem and coming up with a quick and effective solution. When men can do that they feel good about themselves. This causes a great deal of irritation for most women. Women like to *express themselves. They process information and emotions inside by discussing them*. It's not always an issue of needing a "fix"; they just want to be heard. So guys, a freebie: accept that you are married to a grown woman, and she doesn't need you to fix her. Your wife is just as capable of making decisions and doing the right thing as you are. If she really needs your help with an issue, let her ask you! Husbands, you would benefit by being quiet more often and listening to what your wives have to say. Although it may be difficult, just try it and see what happens.

For husbands there is a great desire to *take responsibility* for the relationship. Men want to be the "take charge" kind of guy for their wife and family. Understand that the term *responsible* is in reference to a relatively healthy man. In dysfunctional relationship dynamics where the man has a great deal of baggage from the past, the husband may well be just the opposite and behave in a very irresponsible manner. Women, on the other hand, are quick to *respond and more sensitive to the dynamics of the relationship*. Wives like pouring back into the relationship.

Guys *do it once and do it big*. They invest wholeheartedly for an impacting result. Women *prefer smaller investments more frequently*. An example of this would be the husband who once a year spends money at the florist for the biggest, gaudiest bouquet of roses he can find, throwing in the box of chocolate and the overpriced teddy bear for good measure, thinking this makes up for anything he might have missed along the way. Quite possibly, if you asked your wife, she would much prefer to get one rose once a week on her pillow as a reminder of how much you love her, instead of the circus display described earlier.

Men tend to give of themselves completely. They are willing to *sacrifice it all*, much to their own frustration and regret. Men are prone to leave nothing behind and may resent those to whom they've given it all. If a friend asks us to help them move, we'll say yes regardless of how we may actually feel, regardless of how tired we are or how much we already have on our own plate, and regardless of how many things we have already done for that person in the past. Men are less likely to say no. The reality is that if men do not learn to say no when they should, they may develop bitterness for those being helped. Men spend all day griping that they are now obligated to help instead of helping out of a loving heart. Fact is, they probably didn't want to help in the first place!

Women typically do not deplete themselves to the point of resentment. More often than not, wives can master the concept of *sharing without giving away the store.* This is a simple issue of knowing how to develop boundaries. People have argued the issue of boundaries as being unscriptural. Looking at the Bible, God seems very clear about what he considers acceptable and unacceptable. Are these not boundaries? God calls us to set boundaries so as to maintain loving relationships.

These characteristics delineate a clear difference between men and women, husbands and wives. When all is peeled away, the heart of a man lies in his ability to feel ***competent***. A man has an ingrained need to know that he makes a difference, whether it is in his job, in his relationship, or within himself. The dysfunctional behavior of workaholics defines this very well. For many men, it is much easier to feel effective and competent in the workplace than in a marriage. The job only has a minimum level of relational depth required, and a man can still be effective. It is much more difficult for a man to feel that same level of expertise at home with his wife and family because the investment is so much greater, yet men often feel like they have less control.

The level of depth necessary to maintain a relationship between a husband and wife should be considerably greater. Men can easily get intimidated by the mastery that many women have in the art of communication. Women can talk about anything at any time. For men, it's like the old television series *Dragnet*: "Just the facts, ma'am." Many women can paint a vivid canvas of emotions and responses without a second thought. As men, we prefer to deal with actions rather than show our investment in the relationship through emotions. That doesn't mean men don't have feelings and need to learn to deal with them in a healthy way.

For women, it's a bit different. When you examine the deepest layer of a woman's heart you will find the key issue of ***trust and security***. A woman needs to know that she can trust her husband to keep her safe, do what's right, and protect their family. This is why when a husband does not display the character qualities of a godly man (wisdom, truth, faithfulness, mercy, grace, love, and patience), it disrupts the flow of a marriage and undermines the very foundation of that marriage. Transparency is very important to a woman for it shows that her husband cares and prioritizes the relationship. Your wife wants to know how your day went, she wants to be involved in the household decisions, she wants to see her man take the initiative in resolving issues that need to be dealt with.

Hopefully you can see why it is so important not to provoke your spouse in these very sensitive and very important areas. Wives, do not belittle your husbands; it causes very deep damage. Rather, use this newfound awareness to reach in a positive way the man with whom you chose to share the rest of your life. Edify him. Show him that his presence does make a difference, and that he is important to both you and the family.

Husbands, establish trust in areas where you may have failed in the past. Show your wife that you will be the leader, and a leader worth following. Let your "yes" mean yes and your "no" mean no; be a man of your word. Show your family that you will do your best to earn their trust. You will make your family a priority. Both of you, practice the art of grace and mercy as you strive toward protecting one another's hearts.

> Jesus knew their thoughts and said to them, "Every kingdom divided against itself will be ruined, and every city or household divided against itself will not stand."
>
> Matthew 12:25

When we understand and appreciate how our differences complement one another, God's design becomes clear in his creation of men and women. God's intent for marriage also becomes clear. The differences between us are what contribute to the fullness of a marriage. We can each learn to grow in areas where we are weak and our spouse is strong. The requirement is accepting those differences and coming to embrace them.

Men and women, husband and wife were designed to be together from early creation.

> The Lord God said, "It is not good for the man to be alone. I will make a helper suitable for him."... So the Lord God caused the man to fall into a deep sleep; and while he was sleeping, he took one of the man's ribs and closed up the place with flesh. Then the Lord God made a woman from the rib he had taken out of the man, and he brought her to the man.
>
> Genesis 2:18, 21-22

This passage shows two things: Eve was taken from Adam therefore something in Adam was missing. Eve was that missing something, Eve complimented Adam's life. Secondly, for those who think that women are inferior, note that woman was the final creation, the crowning achievement, if you will. Husband and wife are designed to complement one another as the two form one in marriage.

TAMING THE TONGUE

Brushing up on communication skills is one way that we can enrich our relationships and learn to maneuver the waters of difference. There are several things we can do to accomplish this end. If you examine yourself, you will find areas in which you have used

sarcasm to express your dissatisfaction with your mate. *Sarcasm,*
no matter how fluent you may be, is not an acceptable form of com-
munication. Early in our marriage, my wife made it clear to me
that I had a great gift for tearing her down with the turn of a
phrase—humorously of course. In my marriage, and I hope in
yours, the goal is not to inflict pain on my mate.

My entire life I had been praised for my sharp wit and cutting
remarks. In the secular world this ability drew people to me by
virtue of what today I consider a communication defect. As I drew
closer to God, I felt conviction about this.

> When we put bits into the mouths of horses to make
> them obey us, we can turn the whole animal Or take
> ships as an example. Although they are so large and
> are driven by strong winds, they are steered by a
> very small rudder wherever the pilot wants to go.
> Likewise the tongue is a small part of the body, but
> it makes great boasts. Consider what a great forest
> is set on fire by a small spark. The tongue also is a
> fire, a world of evil among the parts of the body. It
> corrupts the whole person, sets the whole course of
> his life on fire, and is itself set on fire by hell.
>
>   James 3:3-6

James makes no understatement about the damage that can
be done by a tongue that is out of control. This tiny body part
can destroy people with words of anger and hate. This is why it
is imperative to examine what comes out of our mouths, for the
destruction can be devastating to marriages and family.

Needless to say, having asked God to temper my tongue, I no
longer care about the acceptance of the world. What God thinks
of us is far more important. *In displaying God to our families, we*
should do our best to emulate Him. Men, as the spiritual leaders of

our households, that is our obligation.

From the minute we wake up in the morning to the moment we close our eyes at the end of the day, plenty of people and circumstances have the potential to tear us down if given the opportunity. Ask yourself: *do I want to contribute to the "tearing down" process, or would I rather be a part of the edification process?* Our marriages need to be the place where we build up and strengthen each other against the arrows of the world. Are you assessing your behaviors as we discussed earlier? Are you learning to tame your tongue and gather yourself before you respond out of emotion? Are you examining your motivations and responses aimed at your spouse, or are you simply taking everything personally? It is not just an issue of what words come out of our mouth; we also need to consider what we allow into our minds. External influences can have a great impact on what goes on in our minds, which in turn impacts the words that come pouring out of our mouths.

> ...whatever is true, whatever is noble, whatever is right, whatever is pure, whatever is lovely, whatever is admirable—if anything is excellent or praiseworthy—think about such things.
>
> Philippians 4:8

LEARNING TO ACKNOWLEDGE YOUR SPOUSE

One way that we can edify our loved one is through words of affirmation. Merriam-Webster defines acknowledgment as "recognition or favorable notice of an act or achievement; a declaration or avowal of one's act or of a fact to give it validity." An acknowledgment is considerably different from a compliment. Compliments are often shallow and fleeting. "I like your hair" or "Dinner was great" are two examples. This type of validation, although nice, doesn't stay with us for very long. We need to go deeper with our husbands and wives. We need to identify the uniqueness of our spouse, those qualities that first drew us to them. "Thank you so much for defending me to your mother. Tonight I realized that you will protect me and our family." "It really meant a lot to me that you supported my decision to go back to school and get my degree. I know that we are a team and that you believe in me."

These examples go further below the surface of who we are and what our spouse really thinks of us. When it comes to acknowledging, consider the traits and characteristics that God has instilled in your spouse. Remember, these were some of the things you first found endearing. Focus on the things that exemplify and demonstrate their creation by God in His image.

Make acknowledging your spouse a regular part of your weekly activities. The more you meditate on the treasure God has given you in a spouse, the more God will reveal to you.

In the next couple of chapters we will focus on an element of relationship that is often the most cited reason for seeking marital counseling: problems with communication. When approaching something you're unskilled in, wisdom dictates that you seek advice in the matter. The direction offered will be of no use if you don't listen and pay attention. The same goes for interactions between husbands and wives. How we listen and how we respond are key elements to effective communication. Let's examine further as we assess our own listening and communication skills.

TAKING ACTION

Exercise 7.1   A Commitment to Change

Examine yourself and make a commitment: what behaviors will you work on changing to better protect the heart of your mate? Ask your spouse if you are unsure of behaviors that may have hurt them in the past.

Exercise 7.2   *What Is Hindering You?*

Are there things in your life that are hindering your motivations as addressed in Philippians 4:8? Does the secular world have too much control over you? Is television or movies affecting your attitude? Do your unhealthy friends have too much influence on your life? Make a list in red ink (using every other line) of some of the things that prevent you from focusing on what is good in your relationship.

On the alternate lines (starting below the first item on your list) write down in black ink what you can do to minimize or eliminate the impact of those things that interfere with giving your relationship proper focus.

Exercise 7.3   *Taking Time to Acknowledge*

Take a few minutes and meditate on your spouse; think about the traits and characteristics that God has given them. Think about ways they have demonstrated those qualities to you. Write down a few of those qualities that developed into love as your relationship began.

Now that you have done this in writing, practice it verbally. Go to your spouse, sit with them, hold hands, and acknowledge them with words. It may feel awkward; you see we are not trained in such things. Maybe our parents didn't demonstrate shows of affection. Remember, just because it feels awkward doesn't mean it is wrong.

After you complete the assignment, how does it feel to be on the receiving end of your mate's acknowledgments?

Notes to Self—
The Differences Between Us

Chapter Eight

"What Did You Say?"—
How Well Do We Communicate?

If you keep on biting and devouring each other,
watch out or you will be destroyed by each other.

Galatians 5:15

Mark stares at the television, his means of not dealing with
what Sheila has to say. She increases her tone, trying once
more to make her point. "You're not hearing me!"

Mark turns to Sheila with a hard expression. "Are you kidding
me? The neighbors a block over can hear you."

"Being a smart aleck won't change the facts. I asked you three
weeks ago when you'd be able to fix the toilet in the guest bathroom. You knew we had company coming over tomorrow. You
told me that you'd have plenty of time to fix it."

"If you'd stop nagging me about—"

"Nagging? Don't even think about it!" Sheila interrupts. "You can see what happens when I don't remind you: company tomorrow and no toilet!"

Mark turns back to the television with a sigh. "It won't take an hour to fix it." He slides one more remark in. "You have nothing else to do?"

"It only takes an hour? It's been three weeks!" Exhausted with the futile interaction, Sheila adds, "I rarely ask you to do anything anymore. Working up the energy to have a conversation takes too much out of me. You can be such a jerk!" The words just slip out. It's too late to take them back, but Sheila shows obvious regret for her choice. "That was wrong. I shouldn't have done that. I just get mad."

"Join the club," Mark mutters under his breath.

"You know what, Mark, I've been trying. I've been trying very hard. It's like you don't care how I feel. You use words that really hurt me…"

"Like jerk?" Mark says without missing a beat.

"…and you don't let it go. You've always got to have the last word; you've always got to win. You can explain to your guests why we have no toilet in the guest bathroom." Sheila walks out of the room defeated.

You can imagine the scene. Husband is sitting on the sofa enjoying his midseason ritual. It's a close game. The score is 6-7 and a man is on third base, edging to come home. "What's that noise?" Here comes the right fielder, his turn at bat, and the pitch. Ground ball between the first and second basemen, quickly picked up, and the ball is feverishly thrown home. To no avail; the guy on third slides into home plate and is safe! The husband wonders, *What is that low annoying murmur?* The catcher throws the ball to first, again too little too late. Safe! The score is now tied, 7-7. Up to the plate comes the short stop, the guy's got a powerful swing. With increasing irritation, the husband mutters, *"There it goes again."* The pitcher winds up and throws; it looks like it's going to be right in there. The swing and a hit. Crack! A good solid hit. It's going, going, going… *That sound again, like a hive full of bees swarming in my head. Why won't it stop!*

This scene captures what it's like when some wives try to communicate with their husbands. It doesn't have to be an important ballgame, it could be just about anything—anything that's given priority over communication between a husband and wife. We are now going to examine the fine art of hearing and being heard by our spouse.

A variety of issues can interfere with effective communication in one's marriage. They can derive from extended family interference, friendship interference, issues of guilt and shame, faulty perceptions of God, family of origin issues, an ex-spouse, lies a person believes about themselves, and many, many other things. Every one of these issues can cause cracks in the dynamics of communication.

It's funny how many parents demand excellent listening skills from their children yet fail to demonstrate them in their own marriage relationship. Again, we are called to be an example to our children. When your spouse wants to talk with you and share how they feel about a particular issue, show your love for them by making it important to you. If you have something to say, you expect their attention. Agree to talk after the children go to bed, turn off the television, put down the newspaper, stop clipping coupons, *just stop*. Eliminate outside distractions so that you are in a state to hear what your spouse has to say.

Body language says a lot about your interest in the other. Turn toward your spouse, use eye contact, and show your interest. Husbands, if it seems your wife is agitated, take her hand and sit with her. There is a great calming effect in human touch, even if you are the cause of her aggravation.

For many of us who have never spent much time thinking about such things, this seems very awkward. Again, just because something seems awkward does not mean it is wrong. Many of the things discussed here will take time to develop into a level of comfort, but do them anyway. Remember, at this point it's not about doing what's comfortable (that's what's gotten us into trouble to begin with)—it's about doing what is right.

For men, expressing how we feel about things can be a foreign concept. Uncomfortable to say the least. Some men are raised to conceal their true feelings. In fact, our society seems to recognize only one acceptable male emotion: anger. Look at the movies we watch; you rarely see the men in films express emotions other than anger. It's hard to imagine Stallone, Schwarzenegger, Willis, or any of the males represented in movies say, "Please pass me a tissue." Guys, take a deep breath; it's just you and me here. Guy to guy, can you honestly say that you have no other emotions? You've never experienced fear, frustration, anxiety, or any number of other feelings? Of course not!

Men experience the same range of emotions that women do. The problem is that they tend to filter and display their emotional responses through anger, and that way nobody will think they are weak. How weak is that? Let's understand that men are not women, nor should they behave like them. However, many men need to step out of the fear of what other men think and learn a lesson in transparency, most definitely in your marital relationships.

Few men would consider David of the Old Testament a weak example of manhood. From his youth, David's journey exemplified masculinity—giant killer, anointed king, strong leader and motivator, a man after God's own heart. He was courageous yet benevolent, definitely a man's man. David was not perfect; he had many setbacks as well. David was a man of passion who had no problem expressing himself emotionally.

> I am worn out from groaning; all night long I flood my bed with weeping and drench my couch with tears. My eyes grow weak with sorrow; they fail because of all my foes.
>
> Psalm 6:6-7

David was able to lay it all out before God with honesty and transparency. This is what our wives want from us, honesty and transparency. They want to be let into our world, and they want us to be part of their world. Showing love to your partner involves taking the time to listen to them and hear what they have to say.

Trust is only built from a level of transparency. Having said that, we need to understand that both spouses must be a safe haven for communication and honesty. Communication is a two-way street. The sender of a message has to feel safe in *being assertive*, or stating what they want and need in their relationship. You may not always get what you want, but you should have no fear of expressing those wants and needs to your loved one. An example of an assertive statement might go like this: "I realize that you would like to get a hamburger for dinner, but we always go for burgers. I was hoping we could do something a little more fancy, something we seldom do. Would you be okay with going for sushi?"

ASSERTIVE, NOT AGGRESSIVE

A problem arises when we take our mate's communication defensively. This is especially true if what they are sharing is negative—and even more so if it is true. How many times do we hear something that offends us and our listening abruptly shuts down? Many times the other person will say something that triggers a "hot button" in us, especially when the relationship has been on shaky ground. That's when we stop listening and start to riffle through our imaginary backpack and pull out as much ammunition as possible. We lie in wait, anticipating the second they will take a breath, and then we pounce, unloading our full arsenal of defenses against our spouse. It matters not whether what is being said is accurate; we feel attacked and hurt and therefore we attack. *Communication will never be effective if we take everything personally.* We need to practice listening, not defending.

Understand that when someone expresses how they feel about something, *it's how they feel!* If someone expresses how one of your behaviors led them to feel hurt, listen. It doesn't necessarily matter what your motivation was for the behavior (if it involves you at all). Sometimes we hurt people without meaning to. If your husband gets hurt because you didn't get around to reading the paper he wrote for his college class, don't get defensive; it's how he feels. As discussed earlier, just because a particular situation elicits a certain feeling does not necessarily mean the feeling is appropriate, but we can acknowledge that it still exists. Allow this understanding to move you to a place of non-defensiveness.

Each person is responsible for their own feelings and how they behave with regard to those feelings. All too often, the other person takes responsibility for their spouse's feelings. This is why one person, usually the husband, may feel obligated to fix their wives. Even though you may have elicited a negative emotional response in someone, you are not responsible for what they do with it. Our obligation is to do what is scripturally right.

Be aware that there are ways to express yourself without causing your mate to feel backed into a corner. Presentation is everything. When you want to express how you feel in a particular situation, *use neutral words to make the point*, and don't accuse. When you start a sentence with the word "You," understand that now you are blaming the person for how and why you feel the way you do. In many cases, when someone does something that hurts you, they are not even aware of it. Remember, the world does not revolve around you. Sometimes all it requires is the practice of grace, mercy, and forgiveness. Other times you may want to discuss the issue, but be sure to take responsibility for your own feelings.

Instead of beginning the conversation with "You bugged me when you didn't introduce me to your boss. I felt like you didn't even think I was important," try this instead: "Honey, I would appreciate it if next time we meet someone new, you would introduce me. I felt awkward, and I don't want them to think you don't care." You see the big difference in presentation?

Now, when your husband is sharing something with you that has been bothering him, show that you are listening. A great way to do that is to *repeat back what has just been said to you*. Using the last example: "Babe, what you are saying is that it wouldn't be so awkward for you if I would take the time to introduce you. I'm sorry, I just didn't think about it. I'll do better next time." Insert kiss here. This simple response does a couple of things. First, *by repeating back to your mate what has just been said, you show them that you are listening*. That makes people feel important.

Secondly, how many times is there a gap between the brain and the mouth? Sometimes we short-circuit. On occasion when you hear repeated back to you something you said, you'll think, *Wait a minute, those are the words I used, but I don't like the way that sounds now that I'm hearing it back*. As a result, *you also have the opportunity to correct your presentation and restate what you meant if there is a miscommunication*. This simple application has the power to defuse a huge argument—before it gets started. In this way we can address possible miscommunications before they become marital conflicts. It's always helpful to *make sure the message is clear before sharing opinions, reactions, and feelings about the topic*.

During the course of the day things can happen that cause minor irritation between couples. If those items are not discussed and dealt with they can cause irritation over the course of the weeks ahead. Over a period of months, this initial irritation can spread into other previously unrelated areas. Over the years it only gets uglier. It is important to have open communication on a daily basis if you want to keep your marriage alive and thriving. The odds of reaching resolution is considerably greater when these annoyances are still small rather than waiting until they have taken on a life of their own.

WHAT LANGUAGE DOES YOUR SPOUSE SPEAK?

In closing this chapter let's bring together elements of the last chapter regarding differences between the sexes and the communication elements discussed above. There are often key differences in the ways that men and women communicate and show and receive love. Sometimes husbands and wives only communicate in the ways they themselves receive love. These are the folks who complain to their friends, "I don't understand it! If my wife did for me the things I do for her, I'd love it." You see, some marriages operate like two people alone in a room—one speaks French while the other only communicates in German. They both may be talking to one another, but neither understands the other's language. Although they both talk, there is no real communication going on. When we show love only in the ways that make us feel loved, we may never reach our spouse.

Author Gary Chapman has written a wonderfully insightful book called *The Five Love Languages* that helps couples understand how to communicate with their mates more effectively. Whether your love language is *words of affirmation*, *quality time*, *receiving gifts*, *acts of service*, or *physical touch*, learning to communicate in the love language of the other will grow your marriage in ways you never thought possible.

As we look ahead, storm clouds appear to be brewing in the sky. Is there rain in the forecast, or are we headed toward those old familiar gray skies of conflict? For some it may seem hard to believe, but there are ways to avoid continual conflict in a marriage. We need to understand that communication and conflict do not share the same definition.

> Do nothing out of selfish ambition or vain conceit, but in humility consider others better than yourselves. Each of you should look not only to your own interests, but also to the interests of others.

Your attitude should be the same as that of Christ
Jesus...

Philippians 2:3-5

RESOURCES FOR FURTHER GROWTH

Chapman, Gary. *The 5 Love Languages—The Secret to Love That Lasts*. Northfield Publishing. Revised 2010.

TAKING ACTION

Exercise 8.1   Roadblocks to Communication

The following exercise will help you identify some of the impediments to healthy communication in your relationship. You'll note that in the center of the circle lies you and your mate, described as "My Marriage." Take a couple of minutes and write down around your circle the circumstances, situations, people, or anything else that create roadblocks to communication in your marriage.

As you place these deterrents on the chart, put them in proximity to how much impact they have on your relationship. The items with greater impact will be placed closer to your marriage circle (if very severe negative impact you may even put it within the circle), and the items with lesser impact will be placed farther from the circle.

My Marriage

Exercise 8.2   *Comparing Charts*

After you have completed your chart, share it with your spouse and compare charts. Make a list of the *similarities* you found between your chart and your spouse's chart.

Exercise 8.3   *Minimizing Interference in Communication*

It is very important to isolate these interferences and develop methods to combat their negative impact on your communication. In the case of a meddling father-in-law, a solution might be to set up boundaries and limit the family's exposure to him. Another solution might be to have the son sit down with his father and set him straight. What action steps can you take to minimize the impact these interferences will have on your communication in the future?

Exercise 8.4   *Am I Assertive?*

How effective are you at being assertive when it comes to your spouse? If you are not, what prevents it and what will you need to do to change that?

Exercise 8.5   *Am I a Good Listener?*

How effective are you at listening to your spouse? If you are not, what prevents it and what will you need to do to change that?

Exercise 8.6   *Daily Interactions Make a Difference—Practice Assertiveness*

On a daily basis the two of you should sit down together. The less outside distraction there is, the better. You will both need something to write with and on; use a notepad or your journal so you will have it for future reference. Reviewing your previous notes is a great way to benchmark your growth through the years. Sit facing one another, holding hands. Again, the therapeutic effect of human touch should not be underestimated. Holding hands also makes the difficult items of discussion a bit more palatable.

Don't forget to make eye contact, and show your mate that you are invested in them.

Take turns so that the same person doesn't always start. Let's let the wife begin. Share with your husband the negative feelings that surfaced over situations that occurred in the relationship during the course of the day. Focus on the behaviors that caused negative emotions. Remember to use "I" statements to communicate your feelings, and don't blame your husband.

Example of incorrect presentation:

"You are so frustrating! You were late for dinner, and you don't even care enough to give me a call. Hell will freeze over before I prepare you a special dinner again!"

You can feel very little besides aggression and anger in this response. The presentation is one of attack and will put the husband on the defense. If you want to be heard, don't present in a manner that shuts the other person down before communication has the opportunity to begin.

Example of correct presentation:

"I felt frustrated when you came home late for dinner. I spent a lot of time making a special dinner for the two of us, and I would have appreciated a telephone call letting me know that you were running late. I felt like I didn't really matter to you."

This example is far more palatable. Although there are no guarantees as to how the husband will receive the message, odds are considerably greater that he will not feel backed into a corner. This wife is taking responsibility for her feelings without blaming her husband, even though it was his behavior that brought about the emotional response. He is likely to hear what she has to say.

Remember that the husband is free to address anything he doesn't understand and seek clarification. He is not allowed to defend himself against what his wife has said. She is expressing how she feels, and those feelings belong to her, regardless of what the husband feels compelled to add.

Since we do not want to focus solely on the negative emotions elicited during the day, follow up with some positive behaviors you identified in your husband and how you felt about those actions during the course of the day. Again we use "I" statements.

Example:

"I really appreciated it when you asked me to sit down so that we could pray together as a couple. It showed me that you are interested in being the leader of our house. I also liked that you took the initiative; that means a great deal to me. I felt very good about that. Thank you."

If you can't think of anything unpleasant that occurred during the day, do not feel obligated to go on a fishing expedition. Simply end the day by giving your husband a big kiss if he has been a good boy. Being asked to identify your spouse's positive behaviors forces you to notice the things they are doing right. Invariably when a couple in marital trouble comes to see a counselor or pastor, they have no problem bringing out the list of all the mean, rotten stuff their spouse is doing, with absolutely no regard for any positive attributes about their mate.

Once the wife has identified the negative and positive behaviors and shared how they made her feel, she should share something about her husband that she loves. In other words, end the exercise with an edifying comment. Keeping the admiration alive between husbands and wives is a great way to increase intimacy and grow the relationship. You will also note that more positive highlights are addressed through this type of exercise—a good practice for any couple.

Once the wife has concluded her portion of the exercise, it's the husband's turn. The husband goes through the same process. He too concludes his interaction with an edifying comment. Once you both have completed your communication assignment, take your respective notepad or journal and address two things in writing:

1. *What did I just learn about my spouse?*
2. *What did I just learn about myself?*

Having to write down what has just occurred will solidify in your mind how your spouse feels about things and also give you an opportunity to assess yourself. You should consider whether you want to continue a behavior that is affecting your spouse negatively. This exercise, done in a daily fashion, will help to minimize those small battles and prevent them from becoming future wars.

Notes to Self—
"What Did You Say?"

_____

_____

_____

_____

_____

_____

_____

_____

_____

_____

_____

_____

_____

_____

_____

_____

_____

_____

_____

_____

_____

_____

_____

Chapter Nine

Communication and Conflict Are Not Synonyms

A patient man has great understanding, but a quick-tempered man displays folly.

Proverbs 14:29

When we go on a long trip, vacation for instance, we can become hypnotized by the road signs that dot the highway landscape. The ones that typically grab our attention are the yellow warning signs. They come in a variety of styles, but they all signal us to be aware of an upcoming road condition. A common one is the yellow diamond-shaped road sign with the jagged line denoting a bumpy road ahead. We all know what that means: slow down and beware of potentially damaging bumps and potholes. That is good advice when we broach topics that elicit sensitivity from our spouse. Slow down, don't be so quick to react and defend yourself, assess the situation, and don't abandon the thought process in favor of an emotional rollercoaster.

In some of our family histories, anger, yelling, and emotional outbursts were the normal way of "resolving" conflict. As a result, when our hackles get raised we jump into attack mode. Although that may be the default for us, such a reaction will rarely end in a healthy resolution. Instead the battlefield is littered with the carnage that comes from choosing to make winning more important than actual communication.

The first thing we must understand is that no matter what you learned growing up or in your past relationships, communication and conflict are not synonyms. However, for many the anticipated result of communication is always conflict of some kind. But conflict doesn't involve communication; it is simply a case of defeating the enemy. If this is your belief system, no wonder the result is never resolution. In fact, your presentation probably assures that the results will be exactly as you thought. Not because your conflicts need to end that way, but because you create the scene that guarantees the expected result.

Consider this example: if my previous neighbors were jerks and I assume that because of my past experiences my new neighbor is also going to be a jerk, I will probably treat him like he is a jerk. As a result, he will treat me in a jerky fashion. This is a self-fulfilling prophecy that justifies how you feel about the situation rather than you actually challenging those feelings, thinking about alternatives, and creating a new behavior that will lead to a positive resolve.

RESOLVE TO RESOLVE

In resolving conflict understand that *you and your spouse are two different people*; you don't think alike, nor do you always do things the same way.

Offer *grace in those areas in which you think differently*.

Remember that the goal can often be far more important than the path you take to get there. Your way is not the only way.

Sharing suggestions, desires, and preferences will move you far closer to a resolution than making demands and setting inflated expectations of your spouse.

When you engage in a discussion that has the potential of stirring up a negative emotional response, *be smart*. ***Don't even begin the conversation if the surroundings are not appropriate.*** You don't want to end up in greater frustration because you can't honestly express yourself (e.g., the children are playing on the floor nearby or you're seated where others can hear what you are talking about).

Timing is a key element as well. Don't start an in-depth emotional conversation when you are on the way to a friend's birthday party or running late to an appointment. Be respectful of one another. If you have something important to discuss, ***make sure there is adequate time to resolve the situation***. It's not fair for you to just drop a bomb on your spouse and leave them bleeding.

If something comes up that hurts you and you want to make sure it will be addressed, ***ask your mate if you can be sure to set aside some time to discuss what is bothering you***. You don't have to go into detail; simply tell them that you love them and look forward to the conversation.

If your wife tells you this, do not push for an immediate resolve but trust that she has assessed the situation and doesn't want to open up a proverbial "can of worms." Don't you be the one to rush in with the can opener. Just let it be until the topic can be addressed in a more appropriate venue.

When the time and venue are right, address the topic in a way that does not put your mate on the defensive. Remember that when you begin sentences with "You" statements, your spouse has already been put on alert that they are to blame for all the things that follow in the conversation.

If the feelings are riding high and it's all you can do to keep from spewing them all over your partner, that is not the time to address them. Do not broach a heated topic if you are walking a tightrope to maintain your composure. In this state it's usually simply a matter of wanting to vent your anger, not seek resolution of any kind. Your mate does not stand a chance when the deck is so set.

If you are in the midst of a heavy conversation or conflict, be sure to keep a pulse on your own emotions. If necessary, *take a personal "timeout" to regroup and minimize the possibility of saying something you will regret.*

A couple once came in to see me, and early in our discussion the wife told me about her husband's favorite coping mechanism. When the conflict reached a certain level he would simply shut down. He would turn around and leave the house without a word. He would get into his truck and drive off in anger. He would be gone for hours, sometimes staying away all night. His wife would get so frustrated, and nothing ever got resolved. I stored that information until God opened up the perfect opportunity.

A little later into our talk the wife was again sharing about how he walked out on her whenever the conversation got heated. The husband was demonstrating great frustration, and so I asked him, "Tell me, what are you feeling right know? I see a great deal of emotion." He just shook his head. "She doesn't know what she's talking about. Whenever—" I got up mid-sentence and without a word stepped out of my office, closing the door behind me. I waited just outside my office for about two minutes then reentered the room and took my seat. The look on his face was intense. Every muscle in his face was pulled tight. The anger was evident. I caught a look at the wife out of the corner of my eye, and she was beaming. Paraphrased for the more sensitive readers, the husband said, "Next time, don't even bother talking to me if you don't want to know what I have to say!"

I paused for dramatic effect. "Now you know exactly how your wife feels every time you do the same to her." He took it in for a second and then he got it. He understood exactly what he had been doing to his wife.

Even when it is necessary to take a timeout so that you don't lose control and say something you shouldn't, communication doesn't end. Express what you are feeling: "You know, I can feel myself getting angry, and I don't want to say something I'm going to regret. I love you, but I need to clear my head. Please give me about thirty minutes to take a walk around the block (and pray) and get myself together, and we will continue this conversation." Partner, be gracious and allow your spouse the time they need. Don't demand immediate resolution; you will be sorry for that decision if you do. On their return, continue the conversation and work toward a resolve.

> A fool gives full vent to his anger, but a wise man keeps himself under control.
>
> Proverbs 29:11

When resolving conflict *be clear about your desired goal. Stay focused on the topic and don't try to bring in side issues*. Many times we spend more time arguing about the symptoms of a problem than identifying the problem itself. Remember, problematic issues in a relationship are created by a dynamics of two people. Take personal responsibility for your part of the problem. Many times when one person has participated in a bad behavior it's not too difficult to identify equally bad behaviors in the other party that may have precipitated the event. It doesn't make either behavior right or justified.

We all know the definition of insanity: doing the same thing over and over again and expecting different results. *Look for alternatives in resolving problems* in the marriage. Both of you might make a list of alternatives and then sit down and compare notes.

Of all the choices you have listed, *pick one and work together* and see if it produces a better result. Give it a little bit of time to see how things are going. *If the solution you picked doesn't seem to be working, you may have to adjust it* a bit and see if that helps. *If not then pick another one* and give that a try. If you are starting to see progress, don't forget to recognize your spouse's efforts. *Identifying the positive in others goes a long way to ensure that the behavior will continue.* Conversely, when nothing encouraging is ever said, your spouse, who is putting forth the effort, begins to doubt the value of that effort to the relationship and it will eventually cease. Working toward goals of resolution is another way to increase intimacy in a relationship.

Fight Fair!

Presentation can determine whether or not your message is received and acted upon. In conflict management we must be very intentional in how we send our message. Fair fighting rules help couples to stay focused on the positive when there is potential for emotional upset. Respecting your rules equates to respecting your mate. Here are some typical fair fighting rules that have worked with couples in the past.

Stop interrupting. As much as people will say "We know each other so well we can finish one another's sentences," don't do it. When you cut the other person off you show them that you know better than they do what they are trying to communicate. This behavior also tells our mate that what they have to say wasn't that important anyway.

Don't answer complaint with complaint but hear the other person out, and don't try to justify why you do what you do. Again, let them express their feelings.

Name calling is a no-no. This is a juvenile way to end an argument. It sets a bad example for children and only makes you look foolish. Sarcasm and eye-rolling could be put into this category as well. You are supposed to teach your children, they are not supposed to teach you. Don't be childish in your conflict resolution.

Physical violence will not be tolerated plain and simple.

Keep the past in the past. Forgiving someone who is repentant of their past behavior means that you will put forth every effort to let go of your own bitterness and move forward.

> Get rid of all bitterness, rage and anger, brawling and slander, along with every form of malice. Be kind and compassionate to one another, forgiving each other, just as in Christ God forgave you.
>
> Ephesians 4:31-32

Don't counsel your spouse. One of the first pieces of advice in counseling school is simple: you can counsel everyone else, but don't counsel your family! There are many who do not possess a degree in counseling psychology that devote a great deal of time to counseling their spouse. Don't be so presumptuous as to tell your wife what she is thinking. Don't condescendingly explain to your husband his motivations for his present behavior.

Don't preach, even if you are a pastor! Your marriage is not your pulpit, nor is it the floor of the Senate; there will be no filibustering. Be simple, direct, and focused in your presentation of the issue. Once stated, shut up and give your spouse the opportunity to respond to you.

Restate what your partner said. Restating can eliminate an escalation in the conflict because the presenter has the opportunity to correct the message sent if it was inaccurate or misinterpreted.

Be a good listener. This goes especially for men. For women, many times it's just an issue of being able to express themselves. Don't invalidate them by trying to fix them. They'll ask if they need your help.

As stated before, ***timeout is acceptable*** when you explain what you are doing. Even timeout requires some communication so that your mate knows your intentions to resume the conversation once you have gotten your emotions in control.

Be loving in your presentation. Be compassionate and respectful of your spouse and their feelings.

These are just a few examples of rules that a couple can institute in how they will handle conflict in their marriage. You may have thought of some others.

YOUR FAIR-FIGHTING RULES

Every couple should sit down early in their relationship and write out the things that cause escalation with issues of conflict. They should also write out the things that help them to maintain composure and facilitate smooth communication. If you have never done this (many have not) the exercise below will give you the opportunity to do so.

Conflict management in your relationship is not a competitive sport. Don't make conflict between the two of you an issue of winning. If one of you wins, one of you is a loser. Is that what you want for your spouse? Fact is, if one of you loses, you both lose.

TAKING ACTION

Exercise 9.1   Our Declaration of Fair-Fighting Rules
You will do this independently of one another, for this is your personal list at this point and will be unique to you as an individual. Use the recommended rules listed above, but also be creative and add any others that would benefit your particular relationship. You know the things that aggravate you and cause you pain during conflict, and also the things that make it manageable.

Exercise 9.2   Bringing It Together

Now that your list is complete, come together as a couple and present your list to your spouse. There may be many similarities. Using the two lists, construct your own couple's list of fair-fighting rules. This will be your constitution of fair fighting in your marriage. Begin as follows:

Our Fair-Fighting Constitution

We, _____ and _____, resolve to
fight fair, based on our constitution of
fair-fighting rules as listed below.
We promise to uphold these rules to the very best of our ability.
[List rules here]

_____

_____

_____

_____

_____

_____

_____

_____

_____

_____

_____

_____

_____

_____

_____

_____

Notes to Self—
Communication and Conflict Are Not Synonyms

Chapter Ten

Forgiveness Revisited—
The Other Side of the Coin

In chapter five we addressed the issue of forgiving others. Now we will flip the coin and look at the other side: the significance of asking forgiveness when we have wronged someone.

When you commit an act or behave in a way that triggers pain in your spouse, you sin—plain and simple. Your obligation is to go to your mate and make things right. Asking God to forgive you and confessing your sins is just one part of demonstrating forgiveness.

Once someone has asked for your forgiveness and they are repentant, what is the obligation of the person who was sinned against? Look up 2 Corinthians 2:5-11 and read it carefully. I will include the passage here to make sure you don't miss it:

If anyone has caused grief, he has not so much grieved me as he has grieved all of you to some extent—not to put it too severely. The punishment inflicted on him by the majority is sufficient. Now instead, you ought to forgive and comfort him, so that he will not be overwhelmed by excessive sorrow. I urge you, therefore, to reaffirm your love for him. Another reason I wrote you was to see if you would stand the test and be obedient in everything. Anyone you forgive, I also forgive. And what I have forgiven—if there was anything to forgive—I have forgiven in the sight of Christ for your sake, in order that Satan might not outwit us. For we are not unaware of his schemes.

In this Scripture passage, what is Paul saying about the forgiveness of others? We are called to forgive a repentant sinner and affirm them by our show of love. These scriptures were not written with marital commitment in mind, but how much more should we accept forgiveness from our spouse when they have wronged us.

> Therefore, if you are offering your gift at the altar and there remember that your brother has something against you, leave your gift there in front of the altar. First go and be reconciled to your brother; then come and offer your gift.
>
> Matthew 5:23-24

In a marriage, issues of unresolved forgiveness tear at the foundation of the union. It not only interferes with the relationship between a husband and wife, it hinders our relationship with God. We are hypocrites if we claim to love God yet break his command to love others.

Now the true story of a couple who had to fight to save their marriage. Through their developing faith and decision to move down the road of forgiveness in the face of extreme adversity, they truly experienced the presence of the Lord in their marriage.

In Their Own Words: The Love of Forgiveness Received

I met my husband in February 1989. We dated for three years before we were married. I was not practicing any form of religion at the time. My husband grew up in a family where religion was not important or taught, so it was not a part of our lives.

The first five or so years of our marriage were good. We spent the first two years saving for our first home. The next couple of years we concentrated on fixing up our home and getting it just the way we wanted it. Soon after, my husband began a new job working at a small business whose owner was a very strong Christian man. They spent a lot of time debating God, the Bible, and other topics related to spiritual growth and commitment. My husband was always one to make fun of Christians, calling them "Bible thumpers" and "The God Squad." The boss began challenging him to read and try to understand the Bible and God's Word instead of making fun of it. Slowly he began to see things differently.

I was shocked to say the least when he came home from work one afternoon and announced to me that he had given his life to the Lord and was a born-again Christian. I was not too worried though, because I thought that as soon as he realized he had to change his lifestyle and stop doing things like drinking heavily, listening to degrading music, and going to strip clubs that he would be back to his old self again. But he didn't go back to his old ways, and he started attending church.

At the time I was employed as a flight attendant for a major airline. I found myself trying to fly more and more trips especially on Sundays so I would have an excuse not to go to church with him and to be away from home. My husband was also looking for excuses to be away from me and home because it could become pretty tense. He began volunteering at the church mostly because he wanted to help and partly because it meant the commitment to serve would keep him away from home most of the day on

Sundays. We began living separate lives in the same house, and I didn't seem to mind. I felt that he had chosen church and God over our marriage and me.

During this time I began a six-month special assignment job with the airline. Instead of flying trips I was in an office setting five days a week. I was working very closely with a male co-worker. He began saying things to me that I wasn't hearing anymore at home. One thing led to another and I began having an affair with him. I tried to justify my actions by telling myself that my husband only cared about God and his church and didn't care about me. This affair went on for several months before he found out about it. I was out on a trip and at a layover hotel when he called and confronted me over the phone. I had to make a decision in a split second. I could lie through my teeth and try to get out of this situation, or I could admit to the infidelity and face the consequences of my actions. I thankfully chose the latter.

When I arrived home the next afternoon I was half expecting to find all of my possessions out on the front lawn and the locks changed on the house. I was genuinely frightened. He got home a few hours after me. He asked, "Do you want to be with this other person, or do you want to stay in this marriage and fight to save it?" I didn't need to think about it. I wanted to save my marriage; I was still in love with my husband and didn't want to lose him. We began going to counseling on a regular basis, working very hard on our relationship and working through any issues we had. We also learned to be better communicators. We learned the importance of working on our marriage every day and appreciating one another.

Over time, and with lots of hard work, he was able to forgive me. His forgiveness is the best gift he ever gave to me. Forgiveness brings with it a cleansing of the soul for both the giver and the receiver. It is a gift to be truly cherished. Because of his demonstration of forgiveness I was able to grow closer to God as well. I gave my heart to this God that was able to do so much in him. I was finally able to see the works that God was doing in his life, and I wanted that same thing for myself.

I am so thankful that we were able to rebuild the love and trust in our relationship. In October of 2008 an event occurred that changed my life forever. While away at a men's retreat with the church, my wonderful husband was killed in a motorcycle accident. Losing him has been the most difficult and challenging experience I have ever encountered in my life. I take great comfort in the fact that the last years of our life together were happy and fulfilling, and we continued to implement the tools we learned in counseling and we had a great life. I gained an even greater appreciation for his love and forgiveness. I can honestly say that I loved him more on the day he died than on the day that I married him, and to me that is what a marriage is supposed to be.

Some readers may sit back and wrestle with the fact that God took her husband at a time when things were finally on the right track. A great deal of healing had occurred, and they were poised for potentially wonderful things in their relationship. With this situation, I think about a God who knows the plan for each of our lives and the impact he had on them both. It is difficult, certainly at the time, to understand the passing of a loved one. For in her husband I lost a dear friend.

Over time and healing one can look back at the way the overall plan was orchestrated. God knew her husband's time. Perhaps the most loving thing he did was give them back the relationship they had allowed to deteriorate over the years. His wife said herself, "I can honestly say that I loved my husband more on the day he died than on the day that I married him." What a blessing to have their relationship restored. This testimony speaks to the power of forgiveness, given and received. Forgiveness is our demonstration of the love of Christ.

The ability to receive and extend forgiveness in our marital relationship cannot be underestimated. Without its practice, the smallest infractions can fester and become an infection. In Psalm 32:1-5, we find David, a man who made some great decisions in his life and also some bad choices when he allowed his emotions to dictate his behaviors. All said and done, he summed up God's grace, mercy, and forgiveness most eloquently when he offered the following insights:

> Blessed is he whose transgressions are forgiven, whose sins are covered. Blessed is the man whose sin the Lord does not count against him and in whose spirit is no deceit. When I kept silent, my bones wasted away through my groaning all day long. For day and night your hand was heavy upon me; my strength was sapped as in the heat of summer. Then I acknowledged my sin to you and did not cover up my iniquity. I said, "I will confess my transgressions to the Lord—and you forgave the guilt of my sin."

This is our model, this is what we are called to be to our spouse. Take some time and let this passage settle in your heart.

TAKING ACTION

Exercise 10.1   My Forgiveness Letter (Asking Forgiveness From My Spouse)

Since you have already completed your letter of extending forgiveness to your spouse in chapter five, you will have the chance to seek forgiveness for areas in which you have harmed your spouse. Each of you should complete this next assignment.

Return to the earlier assignment in chapter three on selfishness versus selflessness titled "My Contribution List." In this exercise you made a list of your personal contributions to the marriage's present state. Take a few moments to review your list. Now take that list and prepare a letter in which you ask forgiveness from your mate for the things you have done to cause damage in your relationship. Again, set aside some alone time so that you can complete this assignment without interruption. You will use a simple letter format.

First, admit that you were wrong when you did the first item on your list. Secondly, step into your spouse's shoes and think about how it might have made them feel when the offense occurred. Thirdly, write down how you think they must have felt, addressing all the emotions they might have experienced. Fourth and finally, write down the phrase "Will you please forgive me?"

Example:

Dearest Mary,

I have been wrong by not learning to control my temper. I have no right to vent my anger at you in the ways that I have been doing in the past.
- *My behavior must have left you feeling frustrated and attacked*
- *You must have doubted that I could really love you and yet treat you like that.*
- *My attacks must have left you feeling frightened and upset*
Will you please forgive me?

Once you have completed the first item on your list, move to the second item and complete as outlined above. Complete the third, then the fourth, and so on until you have addressed every item on your list, concluding each one with the phrase "Will you please forgive me?"

Take as much time as you need to complete this assignment.

Once you and your spouse have completed your letters, asking for forgiveness, set up a time to meet together. Go somewhere by yourselves; make sure the children have a sitter and you have plenty of privacy. You will take this opportunity to share your letters with one another. When one person shares, the other person needs only to listen and make the decision to accept and forgive. If you are uncertain about what your spouse is saying, ask for clarification. It is not okay to defend yourself, take anything personally, or get angry. Remember, it takes a lot of courage to take responsibility for areas in which you have struggled or failed. Accept your spouse with love and acceptance. Herein great healing will begin.

Exercise 10.2 The Effect of Asking Forgiveness

Once you have completed this assignment, take a few minutes to journal how this experience has affected you and the ramifications it might have on your relationship.

Notes to Self—
Forgiveness Revisited

_____

_____

_____

_____

_____

_____

_____

_____

_____

_____

_____

_____

_____

_____

_____

_____

_____

_____

_____

_____

_____

_____

_____

_____

Part III:

Conquering the Issues That Divide

Chapter Eleven

Money and Marriage

Mark is sitting at the dining room table rubbing his eyes. There are bills strewn all over the table. Sheila comes down the hall and starts to enter the dining room. Seeing that Mark is going through the monthly bills, she makes a U-turn before being noticed. Without removing his hands from his eyes Mark calls her, "Sheila."

Sheila stops in her tracks and slowly enters the dining room. Mark removes his hands. "Sit down."

She sits. "Bills, huh?"

"This has got to stop! You're killing us! We have nowhere to pull from."

"Why do you blame me? I'm not the only one who spends our money."

"You're the only one who's out of control!" Mark redirects his approach. "We can't spend like this. You have eight restaurant entries on the credit card this month alone. I'm not talking about fast food either. When you and Isabelle go out why do you have to buy all the time?"

"I don't. She treats sometimes."

Mark smirks. "Not enough."

"I just don't want Isabelle and the other girls to think we can't afford it."

Mark is taken aback. "We can't. You can't always pay for everyone."

"I know, I know! They are just so...they brag all the time about what they have. It seems like we are always struggling."

"We make it. Sometimes it's month to month, but we make it. Things are tough right now. Besides, I don't really care what they think. Neither should you."

"You don't have to deal with it. Don't be jealous because I have friends."

Mark looks her in the eyes. "Maybe you need to pick your friends better."

Financial dissatisfaction is one of the top reasons people cite for seeking a divorce. A great deal of stress and pressure can result from living in a house that is not in financial order.

Issues of financial instability are more often than not an issue of the heart and not the bank account. As we move forward let's assess your relationship with money. Examine how this relationship affects the dynamics of your marriage. Let's begin by assessing our own individual spending habits. Where do you place yourself on the following spectrum? Rate yourself on a one to ten scale.

Frugal 1 2 3 4 5 6 7 8 9 10 **Spender**

How would you rate your spouse on the same scale?

Frugal 1 2 3 4 5 6 7 8 9 10 **Spender**

You will find one of two things. You and your spouse are opposites in the way that you view money and your spending habits, but have come to a resolution on how money will be spent, and you use one another's strengths and weaknesses to offset your own. Or, as I suspect, you find yourselves at opposite ends of the spectrum and money is a source of much conflict in your marriage.

> When you sit to dine with a ruler, note well what is before you, and put a knife to your throat if you are given to gluttony. Do not crave his delicacies, for food is deceptive. Do not wear yourself out to get rich; have the wisdom to show restraint. Cast a glance at riches, and they are gone, and fly off to the sky like an eagle.
>
> Proverbs 23:1-5

So many people are living from paycheck to paycheck with little regard for the future. It's all about keeping up with the Joneses and making sure you won't be outdone by your neighbor. Having the biggest house, the biggest car, the best outfits, and the best of everything is a driving factor for many. We worry far too much about what other people think of us. We measure our worth by the things we have. These are the values we use to feel good about ourselves. We lose sight of what is truly important. As many are learning in today's economy, those things can be taken away in an instant.

> Whoever trusts in his riches will fail, but the righteous will thrive like a green leaf.
>
> Proverbs 11:28

WHAT MOTIVATES YOUR SPENDING HABITS?

The issue is not money being the root of all evil, the issue is determined by your motivation. The problem is the love of money. If your investment in money is that of status, security, and reputation, you have a motivation problem. God wants us to have all that we can, for he wants us to prosper. More importantly, however, God wants us to be good stewards of our money. When we remember where our prosperity comes from—whether monetary, emotional, spiritual, or physical—we can make better choices about how to be a good steward. Always keep in mind that God gives us what we have, right down to the gifting He gives us to excel in our jobs and be good providers for our families.

Discipline, a diligent work ethic, and learning to be joyful with what we have rather than living a life of jealousy and envy are foundational to financial happiness. Don't spend all your time looking at everyone else and comparing what you have to what they have. Some of the most unhappy people in the world are those who place money at the top of their priorities.

ACHIEVING FINANCIAL EXPECTATIONS

If you and your spouse are not financial wizards, understand that you do not have to figure it out all by yourselves. ***Connect with someone who has more financial experience than you.*** Many times churches have members who specialize in financial planning or offer classes to improve your monetary outlook. There are also organizations that share your foundational moral values that can guide you in financial management.

> Plans fail for lack of counsel, but with many advisers
> they succeed.
>
> Proverbs 15:22

If you don't have the gifting or the knowledge, find someone who does. There is wisdom in counsel.

Don't live on credit cards. If you do not have the money to pay off your credit cards when the bills come, you probably could not afford to purchase the items in the first place. Credit handled responsibly is not the problem, the user is. The interest you pay for extended credit can add up to as much as purchasing the item twice depending on how slow you are to pay off your purchases.

If you have a few outstanding credit cards become proactive in paying them off. Begin by paying off the smallest card first. By paying off the lowest balance first you get a sense of accomplishment and freedom, and this will give you the incentive to pay off the next card.

Once you have paid off the first credit card, apply the amount you would have been paying on the lowest-balance card to the amount you would normally pay toward the next-lowest-balance card and so on. Do not consider yourself to have extra cash until you have completed the process and all of the outstanding credit card balances are paid off.

Following this method will pay off your credit cards faster than you normally would, as well as greatly minimize the interest you would have to pay in the long term. The goal is to minimize the number of credit cards you have and use them cautiously. Credit cards often feed the need for impulsive purchases. Be wary!

Don't be impulsive. If you see something that you really want ask yourself the question, "Can I wait a month before I buy it?" Most purchases are not emergency items. In all likelihood, if given time between initial impulse and making the purchase, you will find that the item wasn't something you really wanted that badly anyway. Also, over the course of that month, you may find that very same item significantly cheaper somewhere else.

Don't spend more than you make. Learn to say no. The worry associated with creditors calling nonstop versus the joy derived from that new *fill in the blank* is significant. Avoid the headaches, wait until you can afford it, begin saving for the item, or learn to live without it.

Don't live selfishly, feeding your own appetite. Once you choose to marry, you sacrifice for the good of your spouse and family. That is part of the commitment. The great thing is that when you live selflessly you reap incredible dividends. You must realize that there are others depending on you and the financial decisions you make. Husbands, you are called to be the leader of your household, but this does not mean you exclude your wife in these financial decisions. Even beyond the family we are called to live generously, not selfishly.

> One man gives freely, yet gains even more; another withholds unduly, but comes to poverty. A generous man will prosper; he who refreshes others will himself be refreshed.
>
> Proverbs 11:24-25

Communicate and work the family budget together. Budgeting is a great way to increase intimacy in your relationship. Whether the goal is to hold each other accountable to your budget or to save for some future purchase, you grow together when you strive for the same end. It is important to keep open communication with regard to finances. It doesn't matter who has the mathematical gift or who actually writes and sends out the checks; what matters is that you are both involved and aware of your debt. Sit down once a month and go over your bills together so that you both are aware of what is coming in and what is going out each month. This way you will be on the same page and there will be less likelihood of distrust creeping in because one spouse isn't sure about the expenditures the other spouse is making.

Trust is a solid foundation for marriage; don't let doubt intrude, especially since finances are a key area that can begin to create uncertainty when things are not going smoothly in other areas of the relationship. This is another reason why I do not recommend separate bank accounts. If the marriage is doing well, do not make the finances the place where you begin to lead separate lives. Again we come back to the issue of perceived trust. Once things start to be hidden in a relationship we have laid the ground for doubt. Since we have introduced the concept of budgeting, let's take some time and create a budget for the family.

WHY YOU NEED A BUDGET

Budgeting is essential to good stewardship. Without it there is no way to say for sure where all the money is going. The only thing for certain is that it evaporates almost as quickly as it comes in. A budget is simply a means of assigning where our income will go on a monthly basis. A budget is useless unless it is realistic. If not we will only adhere to it for a very short time. If we don't honestly assess our expenses we will become overwhelmed and feel hopeless, eventually giving up. You will have the opportunity to complete your own budget using the template in Exercise 11.4.

Some of the things to figure into your budget include basic needs such as rent, mortgage, food, utilities, and transportation. We also want to include things such as insurance, credit card payments, school loans, etc. In order to keep your budget realistic, allot a percentage to entertainment expenses. Otherwise your budget will become more of a burden than a help. Realistically, you will spend a moderate amount on entertainment so you might just as well figure it in.

If your initial budget ends up with a deficit, you both need to sit down and decide which areas you can trim back on, then place the adjusted figures in the future budget column. If you ended up with a surplus, God bless you! You may still want to adjust areas where you feel the expenditures are excessive. Stay with the plan and begin to address the issue of savings and perhaps investment.

One way to begin saving a bit of money is *to keep your*

expenditures the same, and as you gather raises simply put the amount of the raise directly into savings. It's much smarter than raising your expenditures to meet the amount of the raise.

An *allowance* is a great way to encourage some independence. Decide together an amount that will be allotted to each of you for your monthly allowance. This is money that you are each free to spend in any manner you wish. If you want to go to the movies with a friend, go for it. If there's a favorite CD you have been wanting, use your allowance. If you want to save most of the money for a bigger expenditure, save it. The practice of delayed gratification sets a great example to your children. The personal allowance is your wild money. Just make sure that you account for it in the budget. You need to know where your money is going.

Emergency expenses is another category you might want to include in your budget. If you don't use it for a given month, bank it and let it accumulate. Eventually that emergency will arise and you will feel a great deal of relief that you were prepared.

As a couple, decide on *a maximum amount that either one of you can spend without consulting the other*. You shouldn't have to tell your spouse every time you want to buy a coke at the drive-thru or get a burger with a friend. Try to make that part of your allowance money. But since that may not always be the case, you should be on the same page as to what that amount is. For some couples it might be fifteen dollars, for others it might be fifty dollars. The important thing is to pick a specific amount and do not take advantage of this provision.

A WORD ABOUT TITHING

Finally, you will note that one of the items on your budget is *tithing*. This should not be one of the items you crossed out. If we understand that all we have is a blessing from God, it does not seem unreasonable to give back to Him a measly 10 percent, when he is allowing us to keep 90 percent. Tithing goes back to the church to support a wide variety of ministries and expenses that benefit others. Remember, a very important aspect of relationship is selflessness. It's time to start investing in others if you are not doing so already.

> Out of the most severe trial, their overflowing joy and their extreme poverty welled up in rich generosity. For I testify that they gave as much as they were able, and even beyond their ability. Entirely on their own, they urgently pleaded with us for the privilege of sharing in this service to the saints. And they did not do as we expected, but they gave themselves first to the Lord and then to us in keeping with God's will.
>
> 2 Corinthians 8:2-5

If you have any doubts, ask the church administrator where the tithe money goes, and they should be more than willing to share the blessings that benefit others through your investment. I have yet to hear from anybody who is a consistent tither that they have not been able to make ends meet at the end of each month. Quite the contrary, usually God meets their need far beyond their wildest expectations when they are good stewards of their money. Keep in mind that blessings do not just come in the financial variety. We serve a faithful and trustworthy God. Sometimes we just need to give him a chance. You will find that you can't out-give God.

In closing, I want to state unequivocally that I am not a financial expert, but there are a number of ways you can take control of your household finances and spending. Without developing a structure of discipline it is difficult at best to be the good steward of your money that God expects you to be.

TAKING ACTION

Exercise 11.1 My Beliefs About Money

Please explain why you believe what you do about money and your spending habits. Express your spending philosophy.

Exercise 11.2 Spending Motivations

In looking back to the above exercise, take a moment and write down what motivates your beliefs about spending and financial matters. In other words, what drives these beliefs, and how did you develop them? Be honest!

Are your motivations pure and honorable, or are they steeped in fear and dysfunction? Does money bring you comfort? Is money your primary source of security? Does money feed into your self-esteem? Did you find a great deal of selfish motivations in your beliefs? Don't feel too bad. As noted in the chapter on selfishness versus selflessness, it's not an uncommon malady in this society.

Exercise 11.3 Letting Scripture Speak to You

Now let's continue by laying out some healthy motivations for our financial management. Look up the following scriptures and jot down what they speak to you:

Proverbs 13:18
Proverbs 14:23
Proverbs 15:16-17
Proverbs 20:4

If you work on developing the truths laid out in the above scriptures, applying some of the preceding principles about finances will be considerably easier.

Exercise 11.4 Creating Our Budget

The items on this budget sheet (Figure 11.1) are common ones. However, not all may apply to you. Feel free to scratch out any items that do not apply and add ones that do.

The left side of the budget sheet will represent your current budget or where you are right now financially. The right side of the budget will address areas you need to adjust based on what the figures on the left side revealed to you. So the right-side budget will be your new and improved budget for the future. Be brutally honest as you sit down with your spouse and fill out this budget, because if you don't the only one you are fooling is yourself.

Budget For _____

MONTHLY INCOME	Current Budget	Future Plan
Husband		
Wife		
Other		
Other		
Other		
TOTAL INCOME		

EXPENSES:

HOUSING	Current Budget	Future Plan
Mortgage or rent		
Subtotals		

UTILITIES	Current Budget	Future Plan
Electricity		
Gas		
Water and sewer		
Trash Disposal		
Cable		
Internet Service		
Cell Phone		
Telephone (Landline)		
Landscaping		
Other		
Other		
Other		
Subtotals		

FOOD	Current Budget	Future Plan
Groceries		
Dining out		
Other		
Subtotals		

TRANSPORTATION	Current Budget	Future Plan
Gasoline		
Repair/Maintenance		
Subtotals		

PERSONAL CARE	Current Budget	Future Plan
Adult Apparel		
Children's Apparel		
Personal Goods		
Beauty Items		
Other		
Other		
Other		
Subtotals		

SERVICES	Current Budget	Future Plan
Dry Cleaning/Laundry		
Housekeepper		
Pool Maintenance		
Child Care		
Other		
Other		
Subtotals		

MEMBERSHIPS	Current Budget	Future Plan
Health Club/Gym		
Organizations		
Other		
Other		
Subtotals		

EXPENSES (con't.):

CONTRIBUTIONS	Current Budget	Future Plan
Tithing		
Other Donations		
Subtotals		

ALLOWANCES	Current Budget	Future Plan
Adult		
Children		
Subtotals		

ENTERTAINMENT	Current Budget	Future Plan
Date Nights		
Vacation Savings		
Other		
Other		
Subtotals		

MARRIAGE ENHANCEMENT	Current Budget	Future Plan
Retreats		
Book Studies		
Other		
Subtotals		

INVESTMENTS	Current Budget	Future Plan
Savings		
Retirement		
Other		
Other		
Subtotals		

INSURANCE	Current Budget	Future Plan
Auto		
Home		
Health		
Life		
Other		
Subtotals		

LOANS	Current Budget	Future Plan
Car Loan:		
Car Loan:		
Student Loan:		
Student Loan:		
Credit Card:		
Credit Card:		
Credit Card:		
Credit Card:		
Other		
Other		
Subtotals		

OTHER EXPENSES	Current Budget	Future Plan
Child Support		
Education (Children)		
Gifts		
Emergency Fund		
Other		
Other		
Other		
Subtotals		

TOTAL EXPENSES		

INCOME > EXPENSES = SURPLUS
INCOME < EXPENSES = DEFICIT

If you find yourselves in a deficit go back and look at areas that may need to be reassessed. Are there categories that you may want to reduce your spending? You can make any changes you want as you contemplate your Future Plan.

(Figure 11.1)

Notes to Self—
Money and Marriage

Chapter Twelve

Sex and Respect

A s Sheila dusts the books on the shelves she moves downward to the top of the desk, bumping the computer mouse. The monitor, which had gone into sleep mode, awakens with a savage fury. Sheila can't believe her eyes. As the images brighten up on the screen, Sheila feels a sick sensation in her stomach. The naked girl stares at her lustfully. Sheila drops into the chair. Grabbing the mouse, she clicks to view the previous screen, then the next and the next. Her left hand forms a fist as her right hand closes out the website.

Her mind races as she contemplates how she would have explained the images to her young son had he gotten to the computer first. *Has Mark been this careless before? Maybe Alex has seen such filth!* The notions seethe in Sheila's mind as her emotions ricochet like a bean shaken in a tin can. Anger, sadness, frustration, insecurity… She has no idea how she is going to handle this, but she knows she has to do something—for Alex if for no other reason.

Many have an image of God as the old sour-puss prude in the sky. There are some in Christian circles who will not even address the issue of sex, or else they talk about it in such an ambiguous way that you have to keep reminding yourself they are talking about sex. Sex should not be a taboo topic within the church. No wonder so many young folks get all their information from the secular world. God is certainly not afraid of discussing sex, for he created it. God in fact encourages a healthy sex life within the confines of a committed marital relationship. Like everything else in Scripture, God does have expectations (boundaries, if you will), and unlike some of ours, his are healthy. With sexuality, as with everything else, we are still called to be intentional about our behavior, regardless of the emotions associated with the act of sex.

SEX AND THE BIBLE

Sex can be a complicated and problematic issue for some couples. Let's begin by exploring the biblical basis for sexuality within marriage. There is no place in a relationship that self-centeredness is more often on display than in the bedroom. If we do not understand God's intent for sex in marriage, we destroy what was designed to be a beautiful thing. This chapter concludes with a series of Scripture references outlining God's intent for sex.

For more on the celebration of love between a husband and a wife, read the Song of Songs together. This book of Scripture is the most romantic love story ever written. Using this as a foundation, let's address some common issues that have come up.

SHOULD I DISCUSS MY SEXUAL PAST WITH MY SPOUSE?

As shared in my wife's testimony in chapter fifteen, "When Issues From the Past Invade Our Present," it was very evident to Jennifer that her past sexual life could, and in fact did, have an impact on our early marriage. She needed to go through some healing, and I was called to support her through her journey. The information she shared with me gave me a basis of understanding as well as a place of compassion. Now what about you?

If there are issues in your sexual past that could affect your marriage, it is probably a good idea to address them with your spouse. The plan is to share the rest of your life with this person, so don't spend the marriage in deception. Now, in saying that, it is imperative that you seek God in diligent prayer as to what should be shared and what will only produce more pain. Certainly issues of past sexual abuse should be shared with your spouse because they will in all likelihood surface in the bedroom if you have not addressed them through your own healing journey. Again, you are the best judge of what your spouse will receive and what will simply cause deeper hurt, so use wisdom and prayer in your decisions. It might also be beneficial to seek counsel as a couple on such matters. Sometimes having a third party arbitrate allows an unbiased view that either party may not have considered.

ARE OUR SEXUAL BEHAVIORS HEALTHY?

Scripture appears to be silent on so many sexual issues that barrage couples these days. It would seem that by worldly standards, no sexual behavior is wrong. To a great extent this is true. Just take a look at the late-night commercials on television, the magazines available in every liquor store, or the billboards that dot the freeways. Sexual topics are endless. This is not a sex study, but we will address some of the more common issues.

SEXUAL FANTASIZING—WHERE THE MIND GOES

Fantasizing about your spouse is very healthy. Fantasizing about others? This is a problem for both men and women. Men tend to be very visually stimulated to begin with. It's how we are wired. This is a primary reason that we need other healthy men to hold us accountable.

This story will make the point. A young man, early in his career, served as a sales representative for a photofinisher. One of his jobs was to travel to all of his accounts and make sure that everything was running well. As a man, he knew how he was wired, so he created a defensive battle plan. He asked a good friend to hold him accountable because he knew that the odds of participating in questionable behavior when he was hundreds of miles away from home increased. Satan loves to whisper to us, "Nobody out here knows you. How could you possibly get caught?"

Some of his accounts were located in sin city, Las Vegas, and once every six weeks or so he was obligated to travel out there and spend the night. His plan was simple. His friend would call him at about eight on the evening of his arrival, after he was tired and alone in his hotel room—also a time of potential vulnerability. He chose as his accountability partner a friend he respected and would not lie to, someone he trusted and whom he gave permission to speak truth into his life. Over the course of the two years of having to face this temptation, he was absolutely successful, praise God. Accountability is important to both men and women. Just as important is to continually wash your mind with the Word and meditate on what Scripture has to say.

> Above all else, guard your heart, for it is the wellspring of life.
>
> Proverbs 4:23

> Put to death, therefore, whatever belongs to your earthly nature: sexual immorality, impurity, lust, evil desires and greed, which is idolatry.
>
> Colossians 3:5

PORNOGRAPHY—FROM THOUGHT TO ACTION

Pornography is a very dangerous practice to bring into your marriage for a variety of reasons. Let's examine some of the most common.

First, it creates a fantasy problem. We introduce other people into our mind, heart, soul, and relationship. Now there is plenty of fodder to fantasize about people other than your spouse.

Second, there is the moral question of partaking in pornography. The actors/models who perform in these videos or photos are damaged themselves. Many struggle with insecurity and their own need for acceptance. To an overwhelming degree, they come from painful pasts. By supporting this industry, you encourage more of that behavior, as well as participate in the degradation of precious people who were created in the image of God—created for great things.

Third, ask yourself the question, "How would I feel if I found out that my son or daughter were in a porno magazine or video?" We can become so desensitized that we don't even view these performers as human beings. They all have parents too.

Fourth, anything that you partake in has consequences. These consequences can pass down and influence the behavior of your children. Remember, if your children think you are okay with a certain behavior, odds are they will do it in excess.

> You shall not bow down to them or worship them; for I, the Lord your God, am a jealous God, punishing the children for the sin of the fathers to the third and fourth generation of those who hate me, but showing love to a thousand generations of those who love me and keep my commandments.
>
> Exodus 20:5-6

Placing your own sexual desires above God's will for your life has grave consequences. Pornography is a form of idolatry that destroys marriages, families, and future generations.

> ...Do not be deceived: God cannot be mocked. A man reaps what he sows. The one who sows to please his sinful nature, from that nature will reap destruction....
>
> Galatians 6:7-8

You may think that you are good at concealing your indiscretions, but think about it. Is there a more common story than that of the child who comes across his father's pornography collection while riffling through his dresser drawers? God has a way of exposing sin, one way or another. Children typically have high regard for their parents. If they believe that you think pornography is no big deal, rest assured they too will participate in your sin.

Fifth, pornography develops like any other addiction. You see it time and time again in counseling. When you participate in an activity that elicits excitement, a chemical called dopamine is released. Over time, in order to reach that same level of excitement, more and more stimuli is necessary because you develop a tolerance to it. This is true with all addictions. Now it becomes necessary to up the ante. As you become more dependent on outside stimuli for excitement, you become less dependent on, and derive less enjoyment from, your spouse.

Sixth, the more you become dependent on pornography, the less attractive and more insecure your spouse will feel—and rightfully so. You will naturally compare your spouse to the people in the pornography. You may not do it verbally, but you will do it in your mind, and your mate will be very aware of your increasing lack of interest in them. The reality is that people don't look in real life the way they do in pornography! They have been made-up, touched-up, airbrushed, and inflated beyond reality.

One more reason if you need it. Your ability to communicate with your spouse and others will steadily decrease. It's easy to have a relationship with something that doesn't require anything of you. What do you think that does to a marriage over time? If you are involved in pornography you don't need to be told.

In all of this we've said nothing of the secrecy and deceit often accompanied by the use of pornography, constantly looking over your shoulder hoping not to get caught.

If you need any more reasons why pornography is destructive to your marriage, put this book down immediately and go to your secret hiding place. Remove and destroy your pornography collection. Get down on your knees, ask forgiveness, and repent of this behavior.

> Finally, brothers, whatever is true, whatever is noble, whatever is right, whatever is pure, whatever is lovely, whatever is admirable—if anything is excellent or praiseworthy—think about such things."
>
> Philippians 4:8

What About Masturbation?

Here is another taboo topic that is not discussed in churches, probably because it creates more questions than it answers. Over the years there have been many attempts to give the definitive answer as to where the Scriptures stand on masturbation. Deuteronomy 23:9-11 and the story of Onan in Genesis 38:8-10 are the two examples used most often as evidence that masturbation is wrong. Neither of these passages is about masturbation per se. The first is a reference to nighttime ejaculations or "wet dreams." The second has to do with Onan not fulfilling the custom, wherein the brother of a deceased man was obligated to impregnate the wife of his brother so that there would be an heir.

So where do we go with such a controversial topic when Scripture appears to be silent? We can draw some conclusions by analyzing the surrounding issues related to masturbation. This may shock you! There are instances when masturbation may be beneficial to a relationship, such as the very rare circumstance when one partner must refrain from sex for a prolonged period of time, perhaps because of illness. This may be a way of dealing with sexual tension without leading one into temptation. Naturally, we must consider what is prompting the orgasm. If pornography is involved, we already know the problems with that. If fantasy about people other than your spouse is involved, there lies another problem, and it would be sinful by definition. However, if the thoughts are involving your spouse, you do not cross the boundary of unloving behavior.

Another issue involves the fact that masturbation is self-stimulation. The issue of selfishness must be considered. If you are simply choosing to self-stimulate rather than participate in a sexual relationship with your spouse, there is a problem.

Men struggling with masturbation as a compulsive behavior is becoming more prevalent. It can develop along the same lines as an addiction, where you become more dependent on self-stimulation than on a healthy sexual relationship with your mate. In some cases they are participating in the behavior several times a day. Larger issues than simply the symptomatic behavior need to be addressed, such as marital conflict, communication problems, poor sense of self, or other psychological problems. Perhaps an examination of physiological issues in the marriage or any number of other issues that make masturbation an easier option might be warranted. Masturbation is hollow relationship at best.

There are probably as many sexual activities that one can participate in as there are people in the world. It would take several volumes to address all the topics and analyze their value. We've examined but a few.

The big question is, are we displaying loving behavior? Does our behavior lead to peace and edification of our brothers and sisters? As with anything that you do in your marriage, you need to address the issue of respect. If your spouse does not choose to participate in certain behaviors or activities, talk together and find out what their concerns are. If they are just too uncomfortable with the idea you propose, you are obligated to respect their decision. It's okay to revisit the subject, but always be respectful. Everything you do should be motivated by a selfless desire to please your spouse.

SELFLESS NIGHTS

Demonstrate selflessness in sex by participating in selfless nights. Start a new tradition and take turns being the giver and the recipient of the selflessness. It may go something like this. Husbands, every two weeks (or more often) set aside a night to do romantically for your wife what pleases her with no regard for your own gratification. If your wife enjoys romantic walks, kissing and snuggling on the couch, handholding, or anything else that is sexually or romantically pleasurable to her, then do it. That particular night is all about her! Wives, if your husband enjoys going to a nice dinner followed by a night of romantic sexual activity, then do it. That night is all about him!

Remember that we do not forego respect in our sexual requests of our spouse. The goal for these selfless nights is all about pleasing the other person. Being selfless pays off in dividends. As a couple, decide how often you will have these selfless nights. Incidentally, if you start with a selfless night and the spouse being honored is so touched by your display of selflessness that they would like to reward you sexually, don't feel obligated to refuse! Often that is one of the dividends.

Bottom line, with any issue on which Scripture is apparently silent, focus on the surrounding issues related to that topic. Ask yourself the questions, "What is being produced by my behavior? What are the consequences?" Interestingly, the consequences of our fruit are always clearly addressed in Scripture. We are called to love our spouses, and that eliminates the option of selfishness. When we filter our sexual behavior—or any other behavior for that matter—through that prism, there are no topics in the Bible that are not addressed indirectly, if not directly.

A final thought: no matter what we have done sexually in our past, we are not out of the reach of God's awesome forgiveness. Ask and you will receive it.

> Blessed are they whose transgressions are forgiven, whose sins are covered. Blessed is the man whose sin the Lord will never count against him.
>
> Romans 4:7-8

WEBSITE FILTERS and ACCOUNTABILITY

Covenant Eyes: www.covenanteyes.com
X3watch: www.xxxchurch.org

TAKING ACTION

Exercise 12:1 The Scriptures and Sex

We are going to do a little Scripture run and see how God views human sexuality. Write out the following Scripture passages.

Proverbs 5:18-20

The poetry of Proverbs defines the beautiful design of sex within marriage. We are called to happiness based on acknowledging the beauty that first attracted us to one another. We are called to find satisfaction in our spouse.

Hebrews 13:4

We are called to maintain our marital relationship so as not to allow impurity and infidelity into our marriage.

1 Corinthians 7:3-4

We are obligated to fulfill one another and never use sex as a means of manipulating each other. Fulfilling our sexual obligations toward one another increases intimacy and minimizes greatly the opportunity and likelihood of infidelity in the relationship. We must understand that in committing to one another we have relinquished selfish command of our sexuality. We now belong to one another.

1 Corinthians 7:5

Depriving one another of sex should only be done by mutual consent; otherwise we open a door to potential temptation.

Exercise 12.2 Letting Scripture Speak to You

Before we bring this section to a close let's address Romans 14:14-23 and write down what this passage speaks to you. What do you think Paul is saying to the reader?

Notes to Self—
Sex and Respect

_____

_____

_____

_____

_____

_____

_____

_____

_____

_____

_____

_____

_____

_____

_____

_____

_____

_____

_____

_____

_____

_____

_____

_____

Chapter Thirteen

Children—
Understanding God's Gift

Sons are a heritage from the Lord, children a reward
from him. Like arrows in the hands of a warrior are
sons born in one's youth. Blessed is the man whose
quiver is full of them. They will not be put to shame
when they are content with their enemies in the gate.

Psalm 127:3-5

Children are a blessing from God. They really don't belong to us, they are on loan until the day they grow up under our protective wing and we release them back into God's loving arms. That makes the responsibility of a parent of great importance. We are called to raise up and train our children in the ways of the righteous.

Train a child in the way he should go, and when he
is old he will not turn from it.

Proverbs 22:6

My Responsibility as a Parent

It is essential that parents realize the impact they have on their children. Few things are as rewarding as the joy you feel when your little child runs up to you, throws their arms around your neck, and says, "I love you, Daddy!" In such moments they can do no wrong. Unfortunately, life with children is made up of many, many moments, and not all of them are like that.

In order to maneuver through the role of parenting we must first establish a foundation of trust and respect; these are imperative to growing a healthy relationship with children. Trust is established from the get-go. We receive our children as blank slates in many regards. In our hands we hold a tiny new totally dependent being that is counting on us to provide all their needs. These little beings also happen to be very egocentric, thinking everything revolves around them. Rightfully so; that's all they know. When they want or need something, they want it now and they make no qualms about letting you know it. This can be difficult for some parents who don't truly understand the selflessness required of a parent. I didn't realize how selfish I was until I got married. I was used to having things a certain way, and I was never challenged in my preferences or personal goals. I was free to come and go as I liked and to spend my money on whatever I chose.

When I got married that all changed. I was in for a reality check, but this was also true of my wife. We both had to move to a place of selflessness to develop our marital relationship. At times we still struggle with our own selfishness. Well, we thought we had it down pretty well, then along came baby...and baby number two. God took us to a whole new place. We were forced to grow in ways neither of us anticipated. We learned firsthand what was meant by "life is a refining process." Our growth is far from done, and we often find ourselves having to adapt and grow just as our children do.

THE PARENTING BEATITUDES

In the Sermon on the Mount, Jesus describes the characteristics he is looking for in those who want to follow him. These traits are known as the Beatitudes because they reflect how Jesus calls us to be. The following pages present a list of parental beatitudes as a means of assessing your own parental skills.

Be Unified

As this growing process is taking place, the demand for unity increases. The importance of unity is amplified in Jesus' statement in Matthew 12:25, "Every kingdom divided against itself will be ruined, and every city or household divided against itself will not stand." The selfishness of children will run rampant if the mother and father are not on the same page in raising them. Children are far more observant and intuitive than we give them credit for. They have an amazing gift for manipulation. Parents already know that. *This gift for manipulation is fostered in a household where there is no unity between the parents.*

When we are out shopping with our young son Denny, it's not unusual for him to ask me if he can buy a toy. My answer is "No, not on this trip, we are here to buy diapers for Derek." That is not the answer he wants to hear. He will wait for a few minutes, thinking that I am absorbed in my shopping and not paying attention, then go to his mother and ever so sweetly, blinking those big blue eyes, say, "Mommy, I love you. Do you think it would be okay if I got a toy?" Denny's daddy didn't raise no fool. Needless to say, Denny's daddy isn't done working the selfishness out of his son either.

Be Communicators

Your children are counting on you to have their best interests at heart. They need to know you will be available in their time of need. That means you need to be in tune with your children. Develop a relationship that is based on good communication. It is our responsibility to teach our children to be open with their feelings. Children who do not share their feelings tend to make decisions about those feeling based on their immature perspective of the world.

Since selfishness is so prevalent in our society, it is no great leap to assume that the choices they make will be founded in that same selfishness. Do not fear your children's emotions. For some reason many parents shut their children down when they become angry, frustrated, or sad. "Don't do that…you shouldn't feel like that" is a common response. ***Our children have all the same God-given emotions we do, but what is often missing is the social grace in dealing with those emotions.***

When the child's behavior tied to those emotions is destructive, the parent needs to differentiate between the feelings and the behavior that is deemed unacceptable. Make sure you validate the feelings and discuss them with your children. Men (and perhaps some women), for those of you who think that emotions are for girls or sissies, it's time to grow up. That may require you to sit down with a counselor or pastor and identify the reasons you struggle with emotional expression. Do not invalidate your child's emotions; rather consider healthy ways to help them express those emotions. Your children are more likely to communicate with you if you allow them the freedom of verbal expression.

Just as important as what you say is how you listen. ***Give your children your undivided attention when they are sharing with you.*** Turn off the television, put away the paperwork, get off the computer, just listen. ***Acknowledge what they say and hear them out.*** Your job is to be approachable when they need you. Understand that they are children and may not express as effectively as you do, but let them try. This is not the time to correct them or critique their verbal skills. Just like your spouse, they want to be heard.

Oftentimes whether they are heard or not has a greater impact on their esteem than whether they get their way.

A mother brought in her son, a young man about sixteen. She wanted someone to talk to him because he wouldn't open up at home, and he seemed to be carrying a great deal of anger. When he entered the office it was apparent things were going to get interesting. The first thing he did was sit in the chair in front of the desk, raise his leg to the desk, and push his chair back about four feet from it. Arms folded, body rigid in the chair, he was very direct in his communication: "I don't have a f---in' thing to say to you."

It was obvious what he was expecting. This coarse phrase would elicit a reaction and get him thrown out of the office. Ah, he would have to do better than that! I calmly told the young man, "That's entirely up to you. But if you want to chat, I'd love to hear what you have to say." He was very confused, and when he realized my response was sincere, no one could keep this guy from talking! He was thrilled to have a venue to be heard. As he talked more and more, his entire demeanor changed and his body language loosened up. He was able to be direct in areas where his behavior was not serving him productively, and he was eager to listen to what I said.

In the end, after speaking with his mother, it was apparent that his father didn't really connect with him because they never talked. The son never had a voice in the house, and when he was bold enough to speak, his father shut him down immediately. His behavior issues were simply symptoms of a much greater problem: poor communication in the home.

Be Accountable

In the first chapter we discussed the marital roles and how these roles are unique to one another. Feel free to revisit it if necessary. We talked about how the husband and wife are both accountable to

God regarding the issue of submission. Let's address another area of accountability. ***Parents are accountable to God for the gift of their children.*** We are called to raise our children in a way that is pleasing to him. That, by definition, gives us authority over our children. But again we're called to lead our children by demonstrating the character of God and his love. Remember, children model the dynamics that occur in the home. Do your children obey and submit to your authority? Do we as parents help our children to achieve the expectations that God has for them? This may be something for you to consider. The Scriptures have laid out acceptable and unacceptable behaviors tied to God's expectations of our children, many of which you will find in the verses at the end of this chapter (Exercise 13.2).

Our accountability to God is to raise our children in the ways that he prescribes. As discussed in chapter one, God has the best interest of the husband and wife at heart, and he likewise wants the best for our (his) children. Children reap the rewards when the parents demonstrate the same care for their well-being as God does for the parents. So too the children are called to obedience and submission. Children are accountable to their parents (and God) for their actions, and parents are called to be accountable to God in the way they raise their children. (Figure 13.1)

Make your children aware that your parenting decisions—as well as decisions in general—are in collaboration with and submission to God's authority. This sets a great example to the kids and also sends a clear message that the decisions you make will not be so easily manipulated since, just as they are accountable to you, you have higher accountability as well. This is what facilitates the scriptural command for children to obey their parents.

Be an Example

What you do in moderation, your children will do in excess. This statement bears much weight. You must remember that your

The PARENT/CHILD HIERARCHY

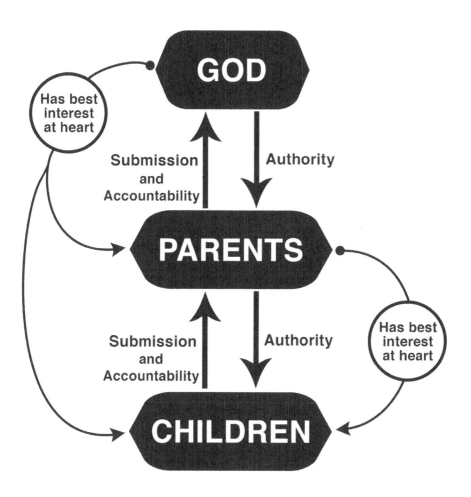

(Figure 13.1)

children are watching you all the time. They observe your behavior and are very astute learners. This is exactly why we are called to be earthly demonstrations of Jesus Christ to our children. Is there evidence in your household that God is the head of your relationship? Don't expect more out of your children than you display.

As parents, we need to be the example of what Scripture calls "unconditional love." That doesn't mean there are no consequences for bad behavior; what it does mean is that no matter what your children do, you will always love them. As believers we need to live by our convictions, regardless of the circumstance. You want your children to be consistent in their beliefs, don't you? Then stop spending so much time in the gray areas. Stop making exceptions to your own moralistic rules, rules which should be founded in the desires of God and not in the desires of your own selfishness. Be a person of integrity, a person of your word. If you tell your child that you are going to do something, follow through.

> For I have chosen him, so that he will direct his children and his household after him to keep the way of the Lord by doing what is right and just, so that the Lord will bring about for Abraham what he promised him.
>
> Genesis 18:19

Our calling as parents is no different from that of Abraham. Even when our children stray in their walk or in life, don't think you've had no impact on them. *Our obligation is to set the foundation for their personal relationship with Christ.* When we plant seeds they don't sprout up immediately; in fact on occasion all outward appearances would indicate that the plant we were cultivating has died, so don't despair. Often quite suddenly we see a bud and that which we thought dead has come to full bloom. Never,

never give up on your children, and never give up on the awesome God we serve.

Be Patient and Realistic with Your Expectations

> But the fruit of the Spirit is love, joy, peace, *patience*, kindness, goodness, faithfulness, gentleness and self-control.
>
> Galatians 5:22-23

Too often parents approach their children as if they were at the same maturity level that they are. Your child is a *child*, so adjust your expectations of their behavior, reasoning ability, and emotional state. Remember, they should not be acting just like you. If your expectations of your children are unrealistically high you run the risk of doing considerable damage to their sense of self. They will feel defeated by the fact that they can't attain the goals you set for them. Feelings of failure are sure to ensue. Be clear about your expectations for your children. If expectations are vague and unspecified you place the child in a lose-lose situation. As with adults, it is vital that children can benchmark success in their lives. If they don't know what is expected it is unfair to punish them when they fail to reach the goal.

In addressing *the issue of rules and choices* for your children, be sure that you maintain some flexibility. Remember that rules should be adapted and adjusted as your children mature. In counseling parents and teens, a common problem that comes up is that a sixteen-year-old is being forced to live by the same set of rules he had when he was nine or ten. It is okay to loosen the reins (your child might say noose) as your children grow up.

Rules for your children should be age appropriate. It is not wise to blanket the rules for a youngster and a teenager. An example might be the household curfew. If a nine-year-old and a sixteen-year-old are required to abide by the same curfew, problems will arise. The older child will feel frustrated and helpless, and rebelliousness will increase as they try to move toward independence.

As children mature, *parents need to increasingly allow them some input into their own lives and to participate in the choice making.* At a very young age we can begin this process by offering our children two consequences for a given situation. An example would be, "Johnny, if you eat your carrots you can have some dessert. If you choose not to eat your carrots there will be no cupcake." This is a choice, and you as the parent have determined both outcomes, but Johnny still has the opportunity to decide. As our kids grow we want them to be in a position to make healthy choices, but this will never happen if they don't have the opportunities growing up. By allowing greater input into decision making, we empower our children and allow them to feel the independence of having some input into their own lives.

> Fathers, do not embitter your children, or they will become discouraged.
>
> Colossians 3:21

Be Prayer Warriors

Be never ceasing in your prayers for your children, regardless of their age. Let your children know that you pray for them, as it sets a wonderful example. No matter what direction your child may appear to be headed, do not give up on prayer. We may not see the results that we wish in the timing we hope for, but be fully assured that our prayers do not go unanswered.

It can be a scary thing to release our children into the world. The evidence of a fallen world is everywhere. Our public schools allow society to dictate moral standards to our children, to the exclusion of God. It seems that at every turn the world attacks the institution of marriage and family through our children. This is why your responsibility is to raise your child in what is right based upon what Scripture says. Do not relinquish the upbringing of your child to a teacher or the educational system. Whether your child is in public or private school, remember that you are the parent. Stay aware of what your child is being taught, and never underestimate your influence. Never forget who is in control, never forget who has the ultimate authority, and never give up on God's promise. Spend more time in prayer and less time in worry.

Be Supportive and Edifying

Your children need your support, day in and day out. Look for the good in your children and lift them up. Make it abundantly evident that you are their advocate and that you have their back covered. Sometimes in wanting what we believe to be the best for our child we can verge on being overly critical. A critical spirit can suffocate your child, so keep yourself in check. Nurture them, nurture their interests, and be involved in their goals. Do not try to force your child to be a square peg in a round hole. This is not to say that you can't encourage them to try different things.

Growing up I was always involved in Little League baseball. I'll never forget one of the team coaches we had. His voice only had one volume. All he did, whether at practice or during a game, was scream and holler at his son. The man was critical of everything that his son did. Apparently his philosophy was motivation through intimidation. The poor kid was doing his best, but his best was never good enough. There wasn't a single game that the poor kid was not brought to tears by his father. As you might imagine, he grew to hate baseball. Don't degrade your children, and don't live vicariously through them.

What about the child who is a few years younger than his

brother and always living in the shadow of the all-star athlete? Comparing one sibling to another is very damaging and does nothing but shatter confidence. Don't expect them to be you and don't expect them to be someone else. Find out who they are, what their giftings are, and help them cultivate that.

Never, *never embarrass* your children or crush their spirit. Keep in mind the sacred position you hold as a parent and the impact you can have on that precious heart.

> Above all else, guard your heart, for it is the well-spring of life.
>
> Proverbs 4:23

Do not let your anger get the best of you. ***Don't reprimand them by yelling and demeaning them.*** Sometimes we treat our children like they are property rather than small human beings. Think about how you treat them and consider: is this how you would want to be treated?

> So in everything, do to others what you would have them do to you, for this sums up the Law and the Prophets.
>
> Matthew 7:12

The best way to encourage positive behavior in children is through *positive reinforcement*. In other words, catch them doing something right. In one household they have a bean jar. They have marked lines up the side of it denoting increments at which their son will receive a shopping trip to pick out a little toy of his liking. When they catch him doing good behaviors, he receives ten beans in the jar. As the beans reach the lines, he knows that he and his parents will be off to the toy store for a reward for efforts well done.

In order to be clear about their expectations of good behavior, the parents cut out little shapes on colored construction paper. They sat down with him and talked about what designates good behavior. On each shape they wrote out different expectations that they have for him regarding his behavior. The shapes were glued all over the bean jar. Their son knows what is expected of him. It works very well and also teaches a nice lesson about delayed gratification. He will not get his reward until he reaches the lines.

Be Flexible

Beware of the dreaded plague called perfectionism, for it can be a destructive force in parenting. Sometimes, in our desire to push our children to be the best they can be, we are overly hard on them. In many cases we nobly proclaim, "I don't expect anything out of you that I wouldn't expect from myself." The question is, how hard are you on yourself? You may need to develop the practice of "lightening up" a bit. Remember, rigidity is a prison of your own making. Practice appropriate flexibility in your parenting and in your own life.

Be a Stabilizer

Children derive a great sense of security from a stable environment. Limit the amount of chaos that comes into their lives by using discernment in what you share with them. They do not need to know everything that goes on in your life. Do not make your children your confidants. In situations where a former spouse is active in their lives, be sensible. Your children do not typically feel the same emotions toward that divorced spouse as you do. That is still one of their parents even though the two of you could not make the relationship work. Always be civil, for that is your responsibility, certainly around your children.

Never badmouth your ex in front of the kids. The children will more often than not view you as the bad guy if you consistently ridicule the divorced spouse. Over time your children will grow and mature. As they grow up they will come to understand the truth about what happened to the marriage, and they will be in a position to make their own assessment. You don't need to guide their opinion to match your own.

Be a Shepherd

The role of a parent goes far beyond that of discipline. We are called to teach, educate, and love our children in spite of some of their behavioral choices. Discipline without teaching is simply punishment and has little lasting effect beyond the behavioral act. Our job is to help them understand why our behavioral choices can impact us in a negative way. My five-year-old, Denzel, was having a particularly bad day, so I had to explain a few things to him. I made it very clear that the problem was his behavior and that if the behavior did not stop immediately he would go into timeout. He chose not to heed the warning, and off to timeout he went. He served his time, and I explained to him why he was placed on timeout. After a hug, a kiss, and "I love you" he went about his business.

Derek, who was two, had been watching the entire event. Some time went by and Derek began throwing his toys. I warned him to stop; he didn't. I looked him in the eye and warned him that he too would have to go into timeout if he didn't stop throwing his toys. He stopped and left the room. I didn't think much more of it. A few minutes later I got up and walked toward our bedroom. Derek was sitting quietly in the corner. When I asked him what he was doing, he said, "Timeout." I told him to get up; I didn't put him in timeout. I kissed him and told him to go play. At two years of age, he was watching and learning about the consequences of unacceptable behavior. Take advantage of teachable opportunities.

Fact of the matter is that *love demands discipline*. God needs to discipline us as adults, and we need to discipline our children as parents.

> Our fathers disciplined us for a little while as they thought best; but God disciplines us for our good, that we may share in his holiness. No discipline seems pleasant at the time, but painful. Later on, however, it produces a harvest of righteousness and peace for those who have been trained by it.
>
> Hebrews 12:10-11

Lack of discipline shows a lack of concern for our children. Although they would never admit it, our children understand that keeping them on the right track is one way that parents show love, because we care enough about them to teach them that behaviors have consequences.

> He who spares the rod hates his son, but he who loves him is careful to discipline him.
>
> Proverbs 13:24

This is not a recommendation for corporal punishment as a sole means of discipline, although there are times when the most direct path to a kid's brain is through his posterior. Spanking should not be, nor does it need to be, the discipline of first resort. The biggest *problem with spanking* is that often it is a knee-jerk reaction by the parents because they have taken the child's offense personally. Spanking should never be administered by a parent who is responding out of anger or hurt.

Some parents are opposed to disciplining their children for fear they will be rejected by them. These are the parents who think it more important to maintain a friendship with their child than fulfill their role. This philosophy is doomed to lead to problems down the road. Although friendships are important, friends are not called to raise other friends. Friendship has a peer quality that limits the degree of responsibility one has for the other. The calling of parenthood, scripturally, goes far beyond a relationship between two friends. Your job is to raise a child who can stand on his own two feet, make healthy choices, and live responsibly in service to God.

There will be a time to develop a friendship with your children as they mature and move out from under your authority, at which point you give them to God. That doesn't mean you will no longer be their parents, it means that your role will now change as you have worked yourself out of a job. Amen.

A Word About Blended Families

Actually three words, God bless you. This is no small task, and you are to be commended for taking on the assignment. The new parent needs to remember that while your spouse picked you, that doesn't mean the children did. A long period of adjustment will take place before you are truly considered a member of the new family. Patience is a necessity. It will be vital for you to develop a relationship with the children. Don't expect to walk in the door and become "mom" or "dad." For some that may never happen. Don't demand that the kids accept you in that role. In most cases there is already someone filling that role; they just don't happen to live in the same house any longer. Do not encourage your spouse to force that role onto the children or they will become resistant and resentful.

As far as discipline goes, it's best to leave the major discipline to the biological parent. That does not mean the new spouse can't collaborate in the disciplinary decisions, but it's best that the two of you do it in private until the family transition is complete, which can take a great deal of time. This can be difficult for the new spouse, but again, the children have to transition before they will even consider you a member of the family. Patience, grace, and mercy are even more imperative in blended family scenarios.

The good thing is that everything noted previously still applies to blended families—just a bit more diplomacy and patience may be required. For you and your spouse it will be important to portray a united front, because manipulation can be a great risk with blended families. This is a topic that can and has filled many books. I recommend that you investigate some of the writings of Tom Whiteman, PhD, who is a licensed psychologist and founder and president of Life Counseling Services and director of Fresh Start Seminars.

There is nothing easy about parenting, so good advice is to follow Scripture as your instruction manual. God is your primary foundation. Always gird yourself in prayer and seek the Holy Spirit for guidance. It is also helpful to allow another healthy couple or two to mentor you through the difficult times. Choose a couple who has already gone through it so you can glean from their experiences. The most important thing is not to do it alone. Your mentor couple can also serve as accountability and help to keep you on track.

> My son, do not forget my teaching, but keep my commands in your heart, for they will prolong your life many years and bring you prosperity. Let love and faithfulness never leave you; bind them around your neck, write them on the tablet of your heart. Then you will win favor and a good name in the sight of God and man.
>
> Proverbs 3:1-4

This chapter will close with the testimony of a father who modeled what he had learned so well growing up: extreme dysfunction. In spite of the potentially damaging consequences of what was occurring at the time, in a very unhealthy marriage, this situation was not out of the reach of God's magnificent redemptive power. This impacting testimony is followed by an email from the father to his son and the response email from the son. These emails were sent years after marital healing had taken place.

IN THEIR OWN WORDS: IT'S NEVER TOO LATE TO BE A FATHER

My story starts like many others. I was fortunate to have both a mother and a father in my home for most of my childhood. Unfortunately, they both were raised by dysfunctional parents, and they carried on the tradition.

My father was a good man at heart but only knew one way of life…hustle. Make money any way possible. This hustling lifestyle came at a cost to all of us. Sometimes he would be gone from the home for days at a time. He would return with money in his pocket and a story to tell my mom. He would make it up to his four boys by showering us with money and gifts. He bought our approval of what he was doing.

One afternoon, I was taking a bath and heard a large disturbance in the house. In an instant the bathroom door kicked open and there was a man with a gun, saying, "He's not in here!" The water in the tub immediately changed colors. I put on some clothes and went out into the living room and found the house filled with DEA agents and cops. My mom was crying and my brothers as well, for they were too young to know what was going on. An informant had told the police of my father's drug dealings. They found my father and he was arrested. We lost everything and went on welfare.

I spent the next five-and-a-half years without a father. I would visit my father in prison once or twice a month. I can still hear the prison doors closing behind me as we went through the visitation process.

I was on my own. I looked for a place to belong and ended up with the wrong bunch of guys. I went to the streets and did all the wrong things: drinking, stealing, and drugs. This lifestyle lasted into my adolescence. I was becoming a lot like my father. My mom had told me that, and I always had mixed feelings when she said it

Once my father was released from prison, we tried to make it work as a family. It didn't last. My father left the house and my brothers and I were again left without a father, my mom without a husband.

I continued abusing alcohol and drugs and living a wild lifestyle. At the tender age of eighteen, I met the woman who was to become my wife. Within the year we were married. My wife was pregnant at the time of our marriage, and we were parents in a matter of months. We were broke, no jobs and no home. We lived in a house owned by my father-in-law and paid rent when possible. I eventually got a job at a pharmaceutical company. I had access to many types of drugs and used to trade for the drug of my choice: cocaine. I was arrested many times on various charges and at least four DUIs. The first two years of our marriage was a shambles. I put my wife and son through hell on earth…just like my father had done to us.

I was so absorbed in my addictions and overwhelmed by being a husband and father at such a young age that I felt like I had to get out. One Friday I came home from work to a home-cooked meal and a loving wife and son, and said, "I am leaving!" I needed to be out doing my thing. It was one of the most selfish things I have ever done in my life. It was devastating to my wife. My son was too young to know what had happened. I packed my things and left. You can see the pattern of my childhood developing in my adult life.

My wife and son struggled to make a life for themselves. I will never be able to pay my wife back for all that she had done. Looking back, the most important thing my wife did for me was to never turn my son against me.

My wife and I began to see each other again and eventually got back together. I moved back in and tried to make it work. My son looked at me like "who is this man sleeping with my mom...that's my part of the bed." Once again, I made life hell for my wife and son. As we tried to make sense of things, my wife became pregnant with our daughter. I had hoped this happy occasion would help change me...no way! I continued my wild lifestyle. Maybe my mom was right, I was just like my father.

My wife met a lady at her job that shared the Lord Jesus Christ with her. Then one Easter Sunday morning my wife went to church and heard the Word preached in a way she had never heard before. As she puts it, "I saw sin for what it is." She accepted the Lord and her world changed. She became an awesome prayer warrior and prayed for me constantly. As I continued in my destructive lifestyle, I had a new problem. My wife was in love with another man, one that I couldn't confront or fight...Jesus! After many requests to come to church, I finally gave in on New Year's Eve. That night I figured I could go to church and would still get home in time to go out partying afterward. Well, I went to church and met Jesus face-to-face. God set me free from my drug addiction. For whatever reason, only God knows, I continued with my drinking and it was continuing to cause marital problems.

As my drinking continued God started the process of setting me free. You see, along with my drinking came my uncontrollable temper. My temper was so bad that my wife and kids were afraid of me. When my anger came on, my kids would literally run from the house leaving my wife to take on the brunt of it all. It got so bad that my wife was ready to leave me. Then one night as we had Bible study at our home some men prayed for me, again for my anger.

God took me back to the source of my anger, my upbringing, and set me free. I came downstairs a new man in Christ. Needless to say, my wife was shocked. She said that as soon as she saw me she knew God had done something in my life. I just couldn't give up the drinking. I was just like my father.

For years my wife and I continued in our walk with the Lord, active in church, put in leadership roles, and having Bible studies at our house. We were happy as far as anyone could see…on the outside. Then a girl from my past called me out of the blue and told me she had been looking for me and would love to have lunch and talk. Well you know the rest, same old story. One lunch led to an ongoing affair that lasted for a while. With this affair my drinking got worse. Sin makes you stupid. Finally, the truth came out.

I went to my pastor and confessed what I had done. The church immediately removed me from any leadership role I had. I was put into an accountability group that was focused on this issue. I had to go to those people that I was giving oversight to and confess my sin. This was one of the hardest things for me to do. I saw in their eyes the bitter disappointment in me. My wife had forgiven me but was in the "wait and see" mode. She wanted to see me change and bend my knee to God.

Then I had to confess to my children what I had done. When I spoke to my son I will never forget the words he said to me, "Dad, don't leave me again!" I was crushed! My son remembered that I had left him at a very early age and was still struggling with that. I did everything in my power to make it up to my wife and children for what I had done. But I realized that I can only do this with God's grace and mercy. I gave everything to God. My drinking had stopped and my walk with the Lord became strong, stronger than ever.

At times I wonder how my son and daughter made it through what I had done and became the wonderful adults that they are. I am a blessed man. I can look back and see where God had his hand on me. We are able to talk to people about what can happen in your life and how God can see you through it all. As we share our testimony of how God restored our marriage and our relationship with our children, we help them understand that there is hope.

My relationship with my children and grandchildren is strong. God has given me another chance with my four granddaughters. My son and I have grown to love and respect each other. My son assured me of our relationship through an email he sent from Thailand while filming a movie. God is good. Now I can say that I am like my Father.

The following are the pair of emails, one sent from the father to his son and the second his son's response. They demonstrate God's restorative power in relationship:

It was good hearing from you last night my son. You know, it's funny when you are home and we don't hear from you for a few days, we know in our hearts that you are around the corner. Now that you are out of the country it sure is good hearing your voice!!!

Everyone at church was glad to hear that you're okay and all is well. They all send their love and prayers and wish you well. Mom and I will be teaching our marriage class tonight continuing on the unit about raising your children. WOW, what an eye-opener for me. I really don't know how you and your sister made it this far. I did not know what I was doing or not doing in your lives as kids.

Son, I am truly sorry for not always being the father that I should have been. God is merciful and has held you and your sister in his hands until I was capable of being a father. Now I hope and pray I can be the father you both have always wanted. I love you son. The stories that mom and I share in the class are testimony to God's mercy and grace and have helped not only the people in our class but have been strengthening to your mom and me.

Well, I am off to study for tonight, so I'll talk to you soon. Have a blessed day and be safe in your God's hands, my son.

Love, POP

Wow, thank you for that dad, it means the world to me to hear it. Although I must admit somehow I've always been numb, or not fully aware, of all that went down. I feel like God's mercy was memory suppression. I can say without a doubt that I don't know how I made it this far either. I do know that your presence has truly saved me from going over the edge long ago. When I tell people about my dad, it's always with amazement that you've survived your own life experiences. It's with admiration that I can tell my friends how proud I am of you.

I reflect at times, even now in Thailand, and say, "How the hell did I get here? How did my life come to this place? Do I even deserve all that I have?" I can imagine that you and I share the same emotion about our lives. I want you to know that I love you as much as any son could love his father. You are my role model and my hero for never running or leaving altogether. You and I both know that would have been so much easier, but you stayed, fought, survived, and was humbled, broken, and put back together. It's an amazing sight from where I stand. I always say to my friends when I want to give up, leave, or take it out on someone else, "If my dad could go through and survive his life, I can not only survive, but I will live my life to the fullest."

I pray that God's mercy will lead you to a completely free place in your heart, that you can fully feel alive and happy with your life. Whenever you're in doubt, stop and look around at the house. The smile on mom's face, your two kids and those grandbabies; see that you are in every one of us, you as the father are the cornerstone of it all. Now put that together with mom's strength and you can see how we all got here.

Thank you for playing baseball with me, I can never forget how I wanted so badly to throw the ball as hard as you. The best part was playing catch with you in the front of our old house. You're the best. I love you, and don't ever doubt that. I have no anger or resentment toward you at all, only love. I can't wait to see you when I get home.

Your Son

Just as we need to reconcile ourselves to God and give up our destructive behaviors, it is important to reconcile with those we may have hurt. Through it all, we serve a God of restored relationship. If you have wronged your children in the past, do not live in that any longer, but make it right and demonstrate God's relationship with you to your children.

RESOURCES FOR FURTHER GROWTH

Fitter, Jay Scott. *Respect Your Children—A Practical Guide to Effective Parenting*. iUniverse. 2010.

TAKING ACTION

Exercise 13:1 Letting Scripture Speak to You

"Train a child in the way he should go" may seem a bit vague to some. What is your interpretation of Proverbs 22:6?

Exercise 13.2 What Does God Expect of Our Children?

We need to understand what God is looking for in our children so we may know how better to lay out the foundation for raising them. Identify the trait that God expects to be developed in our children through the following set of scriptures:

- Proverbs 1:5
- Proverbs 12:22
- Proverbs 13:3
- Proverbs 13:4
- Proverbs 16:5
- Proverbs 16:32
- Proverbs 17:17
- Proverbs 17:19
- Proverbs 18:12
- Proverbs 23:12
- Ephesians 4:26-27
- Ephesians 4:32
- Ephesians 6:1
- Ephesians 6:2

The last verse listed tells children to "honor your mother and father." This brings up a question. As a parent are you honorable? Does your example demonstrate the traits that God wants cultivated in your children? Take some time and look at the traits you listed regarding the previous scriptures. Where do you fall short? Be honest and make a list of those traits that you are going to commit to working on, thereby setting a better example for your children. Face it, you probably already know the areas in which you need work; now be honest and acknowledge them. Ask God to show you these areas, and ask him for clarification on how to change them.

Exercise 13.3 Rules and Expectations for Your Children

Do you think you *free* your children or *enslave* them with your rules and expectations? How so?

Let's get some additional input. Ask your older children (beginning at perhaps nine or ten years old) to share their opinions of the household rules or lack thereof. This is not a wish list for your children that will be fulfilled, just a gathering of information. Jot down what they express to you. This will be an interesting exercise. You may need additional paper if you have many children.

Exercise 13.4 Revisiting the Rules

Now sit down with your spouse and discuss the children's assessment of the rules. Write down the rules that you both feel need to be revisited based on the input you received and your own personal assessments.

Exercise 13.5 Referring to the Word

Take a moment and look up these two scriptures:

- Philippians 4:6-7, what does it speak to you?
- Psalm 34:15-18, what does it speak to you?

In these scriptures we are encouraged not to waste our time in worry but rather invest that time in prayer to the Lord.

Notes to Self—
Children—Understanding God's Gift

_____

_____

_____

_____

_____

_____

_____

_____

_____

_____

_____

_____

_____

_____

_____

_____

_____

_____

_____

_____

_____

_____

_____

Chapter Fourteen

It's All About Me!— Addiction Within the Marriage

Throughout this book we've seen that selfishness can have a variety of faces—identities that some may not label as selfishness. In this chapter we will explore an ever growing category of self-centeredness that is tearing marital relationships asunder. Addictions have to represent the most common coping mechanism in our society. They run the gamut from drugs, alcohol, and pornography to shopaholism and a variety of others, too many to mention. Sometimes they can take on quite a noble air; workaholism is a great example. What could be wrong about working hard for my family? Motivation is always the core issue. More often than not, people who work all the time are trying to escape from their family for any number of reasons. For a man who doesn't feel secure in his marriage, he will dive into his work where he gets the recognition he craves; it's easier than putting forth effort into something he may not be good at—for example, relationships.

In fact all addictions, even where there may be a genetic or environmental predisposition, are determined by the motivation to pursue avenues of escape. After all, not everyone raised by an alcoholic is cursed to live a life of alcoholism. A man (or woman) reared by a workaholic is not doomed to live that type of life, although you may have been taught that such behavior is one way to handle issues you would prefer not to deal with. Predisposition does not mean you don't have a choice about such things. But if a person is not deliberate about their behavior and fully aware of past predispositions, the odds are great that they will indeed become what they swear they will never be. No one should be relieved of the responsibility of personal choice.

Fear of intimacy and relationship can easily lead to addictions to pornography. There is no fear of engaging in intimate behavior with a person printed on a page, or the unfortunate damaged people performing in sex films. You never have to worry about being rejected or measuring up. You can pretend to be whoever you like in your fantasy realm. The problem is, it's not real, and eventually you have to come back to the same issues and stressors you tried to escape from.

For the workaholic, you are always on top, always the best. You put forth every effort to please the boss. The boss can be much easier to please because there is no emotional investment in the other person. The expectations are very clear and the accolades are direct. If you do your job, you get personal recognition or financial rewards. Again, little of it has to do with the uncertainty of relational expertise, which can be daunting for men. Combine that with our manly plague of pride and it creates problems in developing transparency in relationship with both women and other men.

Alcohol is the noble addiction: "Who doesn't drink?" "What's wrong with a little drink now and then?" People make the claim that alcohol helps them to relax. "It makes me more comfortable around other people, and it helps me be who I am and removes my inhibitions. A drink now and then helps me to relieve my stress."

"Drugs are not that big a deal." Have you ever noticed that some people have no problem identifying certain sins as far worse than others? People naturally set boundaries on certain drugs, usually the ones they are not doing, but marijuana, for example, is "not a big deal." "A little cocaine is not an issue for me. I know how to moderate." I wish I had a nickel for every time the person sitting across from me has told me, "I can stop whenever I want to"—whether they were addicted to shopping or crack cocaine.

Shopaholics are a newer identified breed, those who love to go out and spend their money. The issue is not the importance or the desire for what they are buying, it's all about the act of spending, spending, and more spending with little regard to whether they have money in their accounts.

These are but a few addictions, there are many, many more. The interesting thing about addictions is that they are all designed to fill an emptiness, a void in our soul. The root is always selfishness. For the addicted person, the addiction holds a place of importance above all else in their life.

In the marital relationship, addictions tear at the heart and foundation of your commitment. God, spouse, and children should have priority in a marriage. When you light up a joint in the garage when everyone else has gone out to the store, it means the joint is more important than the example you set to your family, especially the children. When you turn on the computer to browse the porn site you've visited so often, you intentionally put out of your mind the pain and insecurity you cause your spouse when they know exactly what you are doing. The damage is incredible.

> Each of us should please his neighbor for his good,
> to build him up. For even Christ did not please himself...
>
> Romans 15:2-3

When we come into marriage we make a commitment to the other person. We commit to be there in body and spirit. We vow to give each other to one another and sacrifice selfish ambition and desires of self-gratification. Our marriage vows do not state that the exception is when things are not going so well or when we simply don't feel like it.

The true healing power of all addictions lies in our motivations to follow the addiction in the first place. We are choosing, selfishly, to meet our own needs, to deal with our pain by not dealing with it. Rather, we simply medicate in a variety of forms, all to the exclusion of our creator. We are choosing to fill that hole in our heart with anything and everything we can get ahold of, when the only thing that can make us complete and heal the pain in our heart is our Lord and Savior.

Let's glean from a couple whose marriage has endured the challenges of addiction and selfishness. They have received the promises God has offered in growing through the pain that self-destructive behavior brought to their lives. The italicized sections represent the wife's perspective of the same time period.

In Their Own Words: Freedom From Addiction

My story begins in the summer, August 8th to be exact. I've been released from prison for all of three months now, incarcerated on drug charges. I wasn't aware of it at the time but I was suffering from post-traumatic stress disorder. I have spent the last four years in some of the toughest prisons in California, and my recent release has presented somewhat of a culture shock to me.

I was on the phone with a woman, and we'd been introduced by my stepmother for a blind date. The conversation was getting awkward, as she was asking me questions you would expect a woman to ask a man she may be dating for the first time. The questions were "Who do you know in town?", "Where do you hang out?", "What do you do for fun?" I knew if I told her I've been hanging out in a cell for the last four years and my idea of fun is going out to the yard to walk a few laps, she would probably never agree to a first date. I decided to let her have it! I told her everything! That's when I heard the crash. I just knew she had hung up on me, but then I heard her voice on the other end of the line, "Hello? I'm sorry, I just fell off my chair." She had quite literally fallen off her chair!

I met him on a blind date, arranged by his stepmother, after a not so encouraging pre-blind date phone call. He had been in prison for manufacturing with intent to sell methamphetamine, with other minor priors to seal the deal. He had four children under eighteen. They have two different mothers, one of which is an ex-wife, and for the cherry on top, the other has a methamphetamine addiction.

During this conversation I was in my office leaning back on my chair with my feet upon my desk. I remember having to explain the loud crash, and the moments of silence that followed, as I picked myself and my chair up off the floor and tried to recover my composure. I heard him say in a very defeated voice, "I understand completely if you've changed your mind and don't want to go out with me." He sounded lost, kind, gentle, and sincere. "I am not without baggage, for my family issues run deep." I agreed to meet him in a loud, lively, packed restaurant with thoughts of a quick escape and no expectations.

The evening went well. We began seeing each other more and more frequently, and before long we had become "exclusive" in our dating. It wasn't long after that we had begun to make all the mistakes necessary to ensure a failed relationship.

Not immediately, but shortly thereafter I felt I had filled my void. My heart overflowed with love and dreams and promises of bliss. I swooped him off his mom's couch and moved him into my home.

Prison is a breeding ground for evil. I used to ponder on the inmates in prison who relied on the power of the Lord to protect them. After all, where was my God when I needed physical protection. You never knew when there might be war declared on you. I believed that I was not worthy of God's love. This lack of self-worth only contributed to my supplemental addiction to alcohol.

During this time my girlfriend and I were living together, and my night terrors seemed to be getting worse. I would scream profanities in the middle of the night and yell at the top of my lungs. I just felt terrified, isolated, and alone; I felt anxious yet I had no idea why. This was quite upsetting for her, to be awakened in this manner night after night. I didn't blame her for being upset, but this only amplified my anxiety.

I began drinking beer immediately upon my release from prison, and by now I was drinking heavily every day. I was doing shots of tequila before we went to bed in the hopes it would cure me of my night terrors. I know now that I was only suppressing my feelings, the fear, and the demons that I would eventually have to deal with one on one.

We were married on my birthday in a simple ceremony. The next eleven months of our life is what I would call "dysfunctionally stable." We were both going through the motions of being a couple, we seemed to be happy, we had the typical fights that newlyweds have, but there was something missing and at the time I couldn't tell you what it was.

We had our "real wedding" on a beautiful yacht in Newport Harbor on February 14 of the following year. My wife and I had made an agreement that there would be no smutty bachelor or bachelorette parties. My father, brother, and brother-in-law were planning on taking me to a strip club; I am not going to make excuses other than I did object, but we boys jumped in my father's truck and headed for the bar the night before our wedding, and we went straight to the strip club! I'm not proud of it but it happened, and it would forever have a negative impact on our relationship.

We'd had a year of ups and downs, but I loved this man and failure is not a part of who I am. I had hopes of a beautiful home, white picket fence, a child of our own, and the Cleaver Family next door. I cried my eyes out the night of our wedding alone in the bathroom of our hotel room. I felt like our relationship had been a constant rollercoaster ride with very steep highs and extreme lows.

In May, just three months after our wedding, I went to court on what was supposed to be a simple custodial visitation schedule. I came home from court on May 6 and informed my wife that the judge had granted a change of custody effective immediately! She had literally overnight become the full-time stepmother to three very young and troubled children. Don't get me wrong, I love my children very much, but we were not prepared mentally or emotionally to be parents at the time. Our marriage was in very serious turmoil, I was spending more and more time at work, drinking beer every day, and only pretending to go through the motions of being a husband and a father.

Once the shock subsided, I thought for sure I could be the perfect wife and mother. I knew I could fix everything for all, if only everyone would listen to me! I had the best of intentions, but those intentions resulted in the rapid deterioration of my marriage.

My husband's drinking was progressing and my sickness of enabling, controlling, and fixing was climbing the ladder to insanity. I was failing miserably as a wife and a parent. I was angry all the time at myself and my husband. I had no love to give these poor children. This was not what I wanted. My husband was at work most of the day and sometimes evenings. When he did come home, he had to sleep off the beer he'd consumed.

For the next six years, the biological mother of my children took me back to court five times and was constantly calling Child Protective Services on us in an attempt to regain custody of the children. The children were angry. My wife was angry, and the children's mother blamed me for taking her children from her!

Approximately five years into our marriage I allowed another woman into my life, and we began an emotional affair that soon developed into a physical one. I was drunk every day, I was mentally and verbally abusive to both my wife and my children, I was having a full-on affair, and I was dancing with the demons in my head and wondering why they only seemed to be getting more intense!

As if things were not bad enough, I learned that my kind, gentle, honest husband who had stood before God and promised to love, honor, and cherish me until death was having an affair with a married co-worker, and he had allowed her to intertwine and manipulate herself into my 15-year-old stepdaughter's life. My husband told me he had married me for the wrong reasons, didn't love me anymore, and couldn't touch me because he wasn't attracted to me. I felt "gutted" like the wild deer my father used to hunt when I was a child, gutted and draped over our picnic bench in our backyard.

Four weeks prior to this I had reached my breaking point with the alcohol. Desperately I had found a hotline to Al-Anon, a place where people who have friends or family members with addictions can go to get help. When I walked through the doors into that meeting I was looking for someone to tell me to leave my husband. I received none of that. Listening to these men and women talk of their experiences strengthened me and gave me hope. I had people calling me and picking me up to take me to meetings when I couldn't function to get myself there. I soon met my sponsor after listening to her story and her sharing for a few months. This brave woman had lived thru similar circumstances and was laughing and smiling. I thought how is this possible? We talked about God and she asked what church I had tried in the past. I told her and she smiled and laughed. She had been attending the same church for years. I knew immediately the Lord was present.

She suggested I try the church again. "God wants a relationship with his child, do this for yourself, if it's what you want." I thought about it and wondered what had happened to me. I realized I allowed myself to become a beaten-down coward. When did I lose me? I began attending church regularly. The more I heard the Word, the more my soul came back to life. This was a miracle.

The next miracle happened shortly after, when our pastor just so happened to begin a series on marriage. I sat there every Sunday alone listening and sobbing quietly while my husband drank himself into oblivion and continued his affair and the kids watched.

My wife began to go to church, and somehow I noticed the peace that she seemed to gain from it. She began to attend regularly and would often invite me, but church was the last place I wanted to be. For one thing I didn't feel worthy of God's love. One Sunday, I'm not sure what compelled me but I told her I was going to church with her, and boy was I in for a surprise! I swear the pastor was talking to me and me alone.

Several weeks went by and I decided to go with her again, and sure enough I experienced the same feeling as the first time! I did start attending church regularly, but one thing I didn't do was change my lifestyle.

Next was a marriage class that one of my prayer warriors suggested. My Al-Anon sponsor said, "Ask him. Just throw it out there, all he can say is no." By God's grace (again) he reluctantly agreed to attend. The affair was still alive as was his drinking, although now he was lying to conceal both. Toward the end of our 10-week class I finally had a breakdown when he chose to go drink and not show up to class.

I went through the motions of attending the classes with my wife and met some other couples who were going through their own problems. I had even been drinking prior to attending one of the classes. The counseling pastor at our church, who was teaching the marriage class, pulled me out of it to speak with me alone. He called me on the drinking and asked me if I would meet with him the following day and I agreed. The next day I had that one-on-one session with him; this session literally changed my life. I confided in him the things that I have done and the life I was living. He didn't seem to judge me, rather he offered wisdom and advice. One of the most important things he said to me is that God forgives me for my sins and that God does love me. It felt as if my soul had just been released from a self-inflicted prison.

He left home one morning an arrogant man and came home that afternoon a believer. I believe this to be the beginning of the recovery of our marriage. From that day forward, we attended church together. I am no longer alone. I have God and my husband by my side. Miracles continue to happen—never in my time, always in His.

I had ended the affair once and for all. I chose sobriety and to this day am alcohol free. I realized that I had been numbing the feelings I had because of the guilt I felt for the things that I had done. When I realized that God could still love me, it seemed to fill the missing spot in me that the alcohol had been filling these many years. Today as a believer, one of my favorite passages is Romans 10:9, "If you declare with your mouth, 'Jesus is Lord,' and believe in your heart that God raised him from the dead, you will be saved."

We have sobriety in our home today, and for that I am so very, very grateful and proud of the man I chose to be my husband. Today and every day I thank God for giving us both a second chance. I know what I was searching for all those years. My void is now being filled with the Holy Spirit. The guidance and the love and the miracles He blesses me with each day are so apparent I can't imagine living void of the Lord's love.

I am very active in Al-Anon and continue to work on my own recovery and my own character defects of which I have many. Looking within is the challenge. Unburying the demons and getting rid of the hardened heart is crucial to my future happiness. Things aren't perfect in my life today. My marriage isn't perfect, I'm not perfect, and my husband isn't perfect. What I know for sure is that the Lord doesn't expect me to be perfect. He gave His life for me so that I don't have to be perfect. A verse that I have come to hold close to my heart is, "With him all things are possible" (Mark 9.23).

As you will note from the husband's testimony, he used alcohol to numb himself to the feelings he had been experiencing from his past. Also note that some of the other behaviors were selfish ways of filling what was missing in his own heart. Addictions are selfish inasmuch as they are ways that a person decides to cope with pain and problems to the exclusion of those who love them, including God.

Those who feel the need to rescue people caught in the web of addiction are also often driven by a selfish desire to be a savior. It is a wrong motivation when the rescuer is driven by a boosted sense of self that comes from the gratitude of those we attempt to rescue. The relationship is one of codependence. We must realize that sometimes when we intervene in the life of someone and cushion their fall by attempting to take on the load ourselves, we may be short-circuiting what God is trying to teach them. Yes, you can love them, but you can't heal them, and you can't make the decision to change for them. You can walk alongside in support and be available for your loved one, but you can't carry the load for them, relieving them of any responsibility for their behavior.

In walking out of addictions it is important not to attempt the healing process alone. God places people in our paths to walk alongside us, to help us be accountable in our decisions. Remember that accountability will only occur when first we admit there is a problem and accept that we can't do it alone. Accept the fact that you have created an idol to replace the love, grace, and mercy that only God can give. Secondly, be willing to put yourself out there, taking a chance and trusting that other people are willing to love and accept you where you are. Thirdly, give other people (people you trust) permission to speak truth into your life. Be willing to receive the input of other healthy believers.

There are many Christian churches and Christ-centered organizations that specialize in groups and counseling that would welcome the opportunity to grow with you in fellowship and accountability. Contact your local church; many have resources and referrals available to tend to your particular needs. Don't put it off any longer.

Only in developing transparency and cultivating fellowship with others can you step out of the darkness into the light and be free of the chains that have bound you for so long. Let God provide the wisdom and discernment about with whom to share. It is important that you develop relationships and allow people in that have your best interest at heart—people who will protect your heart as you begin your walk out of addiction and start to experience all that God can do in your marriage and relationships in general. The process begins with you; make the choice.

RESOURCES FOR FURTHER GROWTH

Alcoholics Anonymous, www.aa.org
Alcoholics Anonymous Family Groups, www.alanon.org
Narcotics Anonymous, www.na.org

TAKING ACTION

Exercise 14:1 Letting Scripture Speak to You

God is faithful in his promises, and he makes those promises to you. Look up the following scriptures. Write down what they speak to you.

- John 10:10
- Psalm 34:19
- Jeremiah 30:17
- Psalm 103:1-5
- Philippians 2:13
- Psalm 107:19-20
- Isaiah 41:10

Notes to Self—
It's All About Me!

Chapter Fifteen

When Issues of the Past
Invade Our Present

It's a crisp autumn evening. No matter how cold the air tempera-
ture outside the car, it's still several degrees colder inside, chilled
by the countenance and obvious distain Mark and Sheila show one
another. Sheila is staring out the passenger side window. Mark is
looking straight ahead trying to focus on the road as he gathers his
thoughts. "You're just in a bad mood."

"I wasn't until I got in the car," Sheila retorts.

Mark sniffs. "Nice. I'm not going to do this, not right now."

Sheila turns quickly in his direction. "Not right now, not ever!
Just trying to have a conversation with you is impossible. And you
tell me I take everything personally!"

"I just asked you a simple question."

Sheila shakes her head. "As if the question wasn't bad enough,
the way you ask it."

"What?"

"You're so condescending, so accusing."

"I'm your husband! I don't have the right to ask you a question?"

Now Sheila smirks. "You don't ask the question to hear my response. You ask it in order to get some kind of confession. Where do you think I went after work?"

Mark grips the steering wheel tighter. "If I knew that, I wouldn't have asked the question."

"Sure you would have! It seems like the more time that passes, the less you trust me."

"Just answer me without all the drama and maybe I would trust you."

In futility Sheila turns back to the window. "Why don't you just say it."

Mark takes his eyes off the road for only a moment as he looks down. Sighing in frustration, he removes one hand from the steering wheel to rub his face, then sighs again.

Sheila seems defeated. "Just say it. We both know what you're thinking. Just say it."

Mark returns his stare to the road wondering if he wants to take this journey. "Sheila…" An awkward silence follows as Mark decides to move forward. "When I was young, about thirteen, my mom…"

Sheila turns her head ever so subtly as she looks out the windshield. Mark has her undivided attention as he takes another deep breath. "My mom had an affair." Mark pauses, waiting for a reaction, but none is forthcoming. He continues. "She almost destroyed the family. It killed my little brother. He thought the world of her. Granted, my dad wasn't perfect either. Workaholic, not very emotional, you know the type. But an affair, come on! I think they stayed together for us kids."

Sheila turns to Mark, a stoic expression on her face. "You don't think that was important enough to have told me before this? How many years have we been married now? I've spent them paying the price for your mother's affair! What were you thinking? Do you know what it's like living every day being accused and judged of things that you've never done? Thanks for the insight, too little, too late."

Mark is feeling some regret for his transparency. "Would you have acted any different if I had told you sooner, been understanding of my insecurity?"

"I guess we'll never know. I never got the opportunity."

No matter what our upbringing, no matter how "perfect" our parents were, there is bound to be residue. We all have the dream of a perfect family and being raised by the perfect parents. We all want what we believe in our hearts and minds that everyone else has. The unfortunate part is that nobody has been raised by perfect parents; they too have bumps and bruises.

Why did Jesus come to the earth and have to die on the cross? Because we needed forgiveness for our sins, and to deny that is to say that the sacrifice of Christ was unnecessary.

> In Him we have redemption through his blood, the forgiveness of sins, in accordance with the riches of God's grace that he lavished on us with wisdom and understanding
>
> Ephesians 1:7-8

As believers, we understand that our world is in desperate need of reconciliation, and that includes you and me. The term *reconciled* is defined as "to reestablish a close relationship or friendship between." The answer to the problems in our personal life, our society, and our world for that matter is that we need to be reconciled to God.

> Therefore, if anyone is in Christ, he is a new creation; the old has gone, the new has come! All this

is from God, who reconciled us to himself through
Christ and gave us the ministry of reconciliation....
2 Corinthians 5:17-18

We have all fallen to temptation and suffered damage through this journey called life. This damage was not always intentional; sometimes it was out of the ignorance, impatience, or sheer folly of our own humanity. No matter how hard we try to do what is right, we inflict damage of one type or another on our children. Granted, we can minimize the degree of damage, but none of us is perfect. Damaged people damage people, plain and simple.

This is not to say that your behavior is the direct responsibility of your parents, for that is not so. As we grow up and become adults, our parents do not bear the consequences of our behavior. As adults, regardless of our background, we are still responsible for our own decisions and we alone will suffer the consequences. We must be realistic about where we come from because this does help to understand why we think the way we do, which may motivate poor behavior if left unchecked. This does not, however, relieve us of the responsibility of our actions. Again, the call to live intentionally prevails.

We need to realize that in some cases our past can have a profound effect on our present. Our past can inflict great damage on our marital relationship. This is something that requires close examination. In the case study that follows, a young couple comes in to see a counselor about some issues in their marriage. At the intake it was evident there was a great deal of frustration in the sexual arena. Both came into their marriage as virgins, having saved themselves for each other.

Regardless, the husband still had some expectations of what their sex life might look like and a great deal of anticipation about a loving sexual relationship with God as the head. He was very curious about oral sex and wanted to engage in it with his beautiful wife. She flat-out refused and became very angry. He was not even allowed to discuss the matter, being made to feel like his request was unreasonable with no understanding as to why. Whenever he brought it up she would refuse sex altogether. He became more and more resentful, and eventually the marital bed turned into a dustbowl. They grew distant from one another. The pain was apparent, and the counselor proceeded with compassionate caution.

The next question was pivotal. Feeling a strong prompting, the counselor asked the wife, "Have you ever been molested?" She looked up at him and her face washed with expressions of guilt, shame, and anger. She bowed her head while he waited patiently for the answer that he suspected would be forthcoming. "Yes, I have," she said, barely above a whisper. "My father." The husband looked both shocked and angry. She began to open up for the first time about this incredibly painful experience. Her father repeatedly required her to perform oral sex on him from a very early age.

As the story unfolded, the husband started to weep as he realized how unreasonable his request must have seemed to her in light of the circumstances. Now he understood what was motivating her anger. It was not necessarily that his request was unreasonable, but for her the pain and emotion that was brought up at the thought of performing such an act was too much for her to consider. It took her right back to the molestation.

PRACTICE TRANSPARENCY

Open and honest communication in the marriage is incredibly important. If things from your past continue to plague you and infiltrate the marriage, it is imperative that you bring them to the table. Be honest and transparent about your upbringing, about your family of origin. If these issues are not addressed your spouse will invariably be held responsible for events that he or she had nothing to do with. You may not blame them verbally, but you will punish them in your actions. Never forget that you are a team and you are to be as one flesh.

> "For this reason a man will leave his father and mother and be united to his wife, and the two will become one flesh."
>
> Ephesians 5:31

This is where the importance of being safe for one another plays out. You each need to be willing to support and protect one another. Husbands, when your wives come to you to share something from their past, don't hold it against them. Don't say things like, "See, that's why you are how you are!" Wives, that goes likewise for you. Cradle one another's heart as God desires to cradle and protect you both. Husbands and wives are not just to be lovers, you are called to be friends.

> His mouth is sweetness itself; he is altogether lovely.
> This is my lover, this is my friend, O daughters of Jerusalem
>
> Song of Songs 5:16

Unfortunately, many relationships started with sexual involvement and the friendship aspect of the relationship was never cultivated. Now is the time to begin to explore and develop your friendship if you have not done so.

The scenario described above between the young couple demonstrates the importance of couples loving and respecting each other. Even though you may have requests of your spouse, the overlying rule of any healthy marriage is that of respect. No matter what the request, if it leads your mate to feel disrespected it is an unreasonable request. This does not, however, relieve the person to whom the damage was done of responsibility in the marriage. Our desire should be to present to our spouse the healthiest person possible. Achieving that might mean pursuing counseling to grow beyond painful events from the past. In all circumstances, never forget to take your brokenness to the ultimate physician. God always shelters, protects, and heals those who put their trust in Him.

> He who dwells in the shelter of the Most High will rest in the shadow of the Almighty. I will say of the Lord, "He is my refuge and my fortress, my God, in whom I trust."
>
> Psalm 91:1-2

Now I would like to present a testimony that hits particularly close to home. This is a personal journey that my wife, Jennifer, and I found ourselves on as the result of a past issue in her life. She will relate the story from her own words. Understand that I am not a saint, not by a long shot. My part of this journey simply required me to acknowledge all that Christ has done for me and to offer to my wife the same grace that God so graciously extended to me on behalf of my own sinful nature.

IN THEIR OWN WORDS: RELEASING THE GUILT AND SHAME OF THE PAST

My journey begins with my son. He is such an amazing little boy. I do not know how I could have made it through life without my little man. I love our relationship, and we are very close. He is a quiet, sensitive young man with a big heart.

I wish this was really how my story unfolds but it does not. I never had the joy of watching him come into this world or holding him in my arms. He was never part of my reality because twelve years ago I became pregnant, and instead of keeping him I chose to end his life by having an abortion.

If you were like me, you felt shame every time someone talked about abortion. I was worried that someone was going to discover my secret, and I carried it with me for years before I could open up and share my story with other women.

No one made a big deal out of it. So I must be doing the right thing, I thought. Once I told my doctor I was pregnant it seemed like this choice was the next step in the process. It was even a fairly inexpensive solution. It was a small price to pay for a huge mistake. My friends at the time seemed so supportive. They were telling me that I was making the right decision.

I arrived at the clinic that day and was moved through the abortion mill like product through a factory. After the "procedure" I found myself lying next to a line of women that had just done the same. I got dressed and left. It was on that ride home that I felt the depth of the pain inside my heart.

It is amazing how this one incident had an effect on how I viewed the world around me for the rest of my life. There were so many unexplained emotions that would spring up when just the topic of abortion was brought up. I wanted to cry every time I saw a child that would be the age of my child. I wanted to reach out to women that were contemplating abortion, but who was I to tell them not to go through with it. Anger, fear, depression, shame, and so much more seemed to surface in my life at different times and I did not know why. I could never reveal my true self because of what I had done. There was always that deep, dark secret.

Fast forward a few years and I become a Christian. I take to heart the fact that I am saved, but somewhere deep down inside I know what I have done and wonder how I could ever be forgiven of that sin. I finally meet my wonderful husband, and I can't believe how lucky I am to get such an amazing, godly man. I keep waiting for him to realize who he is dating and to run the other direction. God calls me to share the experience of my abortion with him. I expect him to end the relationship…but with the revelation of my shameful secret he responds by telling me he loves me and that he knows I'm not the same person I used to be. We get married.

Being a pastor's wife, I wonder if I am worthy of this position. We try to have children, and nothing happens. It's a difficult time. I just can't get pregnant. Finally, we see a doctor and she tells us that it is nearly impossible for me to get pregnant. The shoe that I had been waiting to drop finally fell—this time punishing not only me but my wonderful husband as well.

My past decision affected the relationship between my husband and I for many years. I did not feel worthy enough to be his wife, and that insecurity put a damper on how we related to one another. This fear caused me to be controlling in my marriage, because I figured if I had control then nothing bad could happen. This was not fair to my husband. I had a gaping hole in my heart, and no matter what he tried to do to help, it was something that I needed to bring to the Lord.

This was a major wedge in our marriage. From month to month, our life would be a continuous emotional rollercoaster. I would hope, thinking that I might get pregnant this month, and then when I realized I wasn't, my emotions would come barreling down on me. My husband had to live as if he were walking on eggshells because of my constant state of emotional distress. I kept blaming all of our problems on myself because I really thought it was my fault, my punishment, that we couldn't get pregnant. I blamed myself but I took it out on the person that was closest to me, my husband. My mind was constantly attacked with lies. Anything my husband said I took personally, as if he too were punishing me for what I had done or who I was.

In order for God to heal this deep wound inside of my heart I needed to take that first step. I needed to realize that he was not going to take me on this journey only to dump me at an extremely vulnerable time in my life. Through a powerful prayer time with a group of women from my church I realized I needed to join our post-abortion Bible study. It was hard for me to take that step. My shame almost held me back, but it would have robbed me of a healing that my heart so desperately needed.

I was finally able to mourn the loss of my precious boy James. Every step of the way I felt God carrying me. He gave me a very powerful scripture that helped with the process.

> To appoint unto them that mourn in Zion, to give unto them beauty for ashes, the oil of joy for mourning, the garment of praise for the spirit of heaviness. That they might be called trees of righteousness, the planting of the Lord that he might be glorified.
>
> Isaiah 61:3 KJV

We serve a God that can take the ashes of our lives and turn them into life. Our healing can be used to glorify the Lord. I thought that he was punishing me for my past by not blessing me with children, but God came through. When the doctors said "NO" the Lord said "YES"! He not only blessed us once, but we have two amazing little boys that are the joys of our lives. I was able to work through my hurts and become the wife that my husband needed me to be.

I have a picture in my mind of my three boys. They are sitting side by side on the couch watching television together. My youngest is in my oldest's arms, staring not at the picture on the screen but into the face of his older brother. He is smiling from ear to ear. My middle son is sucking his thumb and resting his head on big brother's shoulder. This picture in my mind reveals a trio of brothers that will look out for each other and love each other always.

I know that I will not be able to experience the pleasure of seeing this here on earth. One day my boys will meet their oldest brother and they will have the chance to love him. I also know that I serve a faithful God. He is so faithful and forgiving that I will see my boy in heaven, and he will not hate me for what I have done. He will love me and be so very glad to see his mama. When I had that abortion, God ushered my child immediately into heaven. But God grieved for me and the pain I would endure from that day forward. God eventually healed my heart. If you share a similar story, God wants to heal your heart too.

So you see, if left unchecked or ignored the pain from past trauma and unresolved issues can creep right up into your present and take root in your marriage. For those of you who are interested in learning more about my wife's journey of healing, her book *Up from the Ashes: A Handbook for Healing* is listed as a resource at the end of this chapter.

RESOURCES FOR FURTHER GROWTH

Disney, Jennifer. *Up from the Ashes: A Handbook for Healing*. iUniverse. 2010. (Women's Post-Abortion)

Harper, Sheila. *SaveOne: A Guide to Emotional Healing After Abortion*. 2003. www.save one.org.

Harper, Sheila. *SaveOne: The Men's Study*. 2004. www.save one. org. (Men's Post-Abortion)

TAKING ACTION

Exercise 15.1 Writing Your Personal Testimony

Now it's time to write out your own personal testimony. Write out the details of where you come from, what you have experienced, and how incidents in your life have affected you. You may find issues from your own life that you need to forgive in yourself or in others. This is not an exercise in speed so take as much time as you need, several days if necessary. Allow yourself the time to grieve events you may have ignored for years. That is absolutely okay. As you write, you may find it helpful to envision Jesus sitting right there with you, offering comfort and consolation as you revisit some incidents that may have caused you great pain. This exercise may be very difficult for some, and you may be reluctant to go back to the past. However, if you have not acknowledged these events or given them proper perspective, present events will trigger emotions tied to these past events. As much as you may try to stuff these things, unless dealt with they will seep into your relationship and your spouse may not understand your emotional responses to certain situations.

Share your testimony with your spouse if you have not already done so. It is important for your mate to know and understand your perception of the world, based on where you come from. As you share your testimonies with one another, simply listen to the heart of your spouse. Remember that your testimony is not an excuse to continue in bad behavior. Your obligation is to pursue the help necessary to move forward in your life. Write it out in a separate notebook, diary, or journal. Use as much paper as you need and take as much time as necessary. Don't feel like you need to get this all finished in one sitting. In all likelihood, there will be a great deal of emotion attached to this assignment.

Notes to Self—
When Issues From the Past Invade Our Present

_____

_____

_____

_____

_____

_____

_____

_____

_____

_____

_____

_____

_____

_____

_____

_____

_____

_____

_____

_____

_____

_____

In Conclusion

Be Encouraged!

As our journey comes to an end, let's review some key elements that demonstrate the practice of love. A key component in revitalizing your marriage is the understanding that *your marriage is not about you*. Realize that God has created uniqueness in both of you. The more you come to accept and love the differences between the two of you, the sooner you can learn to let go of the little stuff that the enemy loves to use to distract you from the goal. The goal of every couple should be to live for the other, to live for God. That doesn't mean you sacrifice your individuality; it means that consideration for what is most beneficial to your relationship will outweigh what is solely beneficial to you individually. From that you will begin to reap increasing dividends.

Creating a richer, fuller marriage begins with a decision: the decision to die to oneself. This is not only in relationship to God, but also in our relationship to one another. Whether our dysfunction stems from attitudes, behaviors, past experiences, or simply choosing to believe the lies of the enemy, it is essential that we step out of ourselves and move into alignment with our creator.

As you continue on your journey of marriage, begin to step out of the shame and guilt of the past. No matter what you may have done, no matter what you may have partaken in, you are not out of redemption's grasp.

> For he has rescued us from the dominion of darkness and brought us into the kingdom of the Son he loves, in whom we have redemption, the forgiveness of sins.
>
> Colossians 1:13-14

Be comforted; your past doesn't have to be a blueprint for your future. The time to start living intentionally is right now. Let your marriage be an example that glorifies God. The benefits of such a decision are countless, not just to you, but to your children, future generations, and everyone you come into contact with.

> Above all, love each other deeply, because love covers over a multitude of sins. Offer hospitality to one another without grumbling. Each one should use whatever gift he has received to serve others, faithfully administering God's grace in its various forms. If anyone speaks, he should do it as one speaking the very words of God. If anyone serves, he should do it with the strength God provides, so that in all things God may be praised through Jesus Christ. To him be the glory and the power for ever and ever. Amen.
>
> 1 Peter 4:8-11

Sheila and Mark had a good idea of what was expected from them to make their relationship work. Where they lacked was in the investment in one another. Their consistency was sporadic at best. Choosing not to exercise the grace and mercy God had shown them prevented wounds of the past from healing. Not developing or simply ignoring the communication skills that benefit marriage caused further erosion in their marriage. This marital disaster was avoidable; it only required the original commitment that they both agreed upon in their marriage ceremony. Their heartfelt vows contained the following pledge: *I choose you to be my wedded spouse; to have and to hold; from this day forward; for better or worse; for richer or poorer; in good times or in bad; to love and to cherish; to pray with; and to serve God with; for as long as we both shall live.* This, unfortunately, was not to be the case with Mark and Sheila as they moved toward divorce proceedings. As seen throughout the testimonies scattered among these pages, making your marriage work is a choice.

We have addressed many things throughout this book, and the goal was to offer you a foundation for enhancing your marriage. The entire purpose has been to arm you with the necessary tools to attain success in your relationship. Revisit often the meditation verses in chapter one as you move toward healing your marriage. Commit them to your mind, heart, and spirit as gentle reminders of the hope and faith God offers you, individually and as a couple.

If this book has enticed and encouraged you to put forth the effort necessary to achieve the marriage God has for you, regardless of the attacks you have endured in the past, then I have been blessed.

May God bless you both on your journey.

TAKING ACTION

Closing Exercise: How You Can Show Me That You Love Me

Each spouse is to make a list of twenty-five ways that your mate can make you feel loved. These items should be specific and of a positive nature. Don't clutter your list with a series of things you *do not* want your spouse to do. Instead, look at positive behaviors that show you love. It's always helpful to keep the requests inexpensive and relatively simple to complete.

Make a copy of your list and exchange it with your spouse. Sit down and discuss the list with one another so that you are both clear about the requests. Do not present your list in a demanding tone, for these are requests at this point. Now the mission for each spouse is simple: begin to work on your list. You are not expected to complete the list all at once, and there is nothing wrong with doing some of the items more than once. In your hand you now have a punch list that can be used to show your spouse just how much you love them. As one spouse takes the initiative and completes items on the list, it would behoove the other to acknowledge their efforts.

Recommended Additional Resources for Growth and Understanding

American Association of Christian Counselors (AACC) for Christian individual and marital counseling in your area. Contact: www.aacc.net

Kendrick, Stephen and Alex. *The Love Dare*. B&H Publishing Group. 2008.

Author's Biography

Eric A. Disney is a Recovery and Personal Growth pastor at a local church in Norco, California, where he has served for two decades. He is a counseling psychology graduate from California Baptist University in Riverside, California. His ministry covers a wide variety of healing issues including addiction recovery, post-abortion healing, sexual healing, and many others, and he offers a broad range of marriage, family, and relationship counseling classes and seminars. Eric conducts premarital counseling and has developed marriage classes for couples experiencing severe marital difficulties as well as those looking for marriage enrichment, both with a great deal of success. His passion for seeing people healed and marriages flourish has led to the development and implementation of several classes offered to the community. Eric has been an active member of the American Association of Christian Counselors since 1999. He is happily married to his wonderful wife, Jennifer, an author and teacher who is also very active in recovery ministry. Together they are the proud parents of two boys.

CPSIA information can be obtained at www.ICGtesting.com
Printed in the USA
BVOW08s0201140814

362798BV00003B/6/P